Conference Papers Series
No. 14

World Improvised Verse Singing

Edited by Xabier Irujo

Center for Basque Studies Press
University of Nevada, Reno

This book was published with the generous support of the Basque government

William A. Douglass Center for Basque Studies
University of Nevada, Reno

Conference Papers Series, no. 14
Series Editor: Xabier Irujo
Center for Basque Studies
University of Nevada, Reno
Reno, Nevada 89557
http://basque.unr.edu

Cover photo by Conny Beyreuther, courtesy of Xenpelar Dokumentazio Zentroa

Library of Congress Cataloging-in-Publication Data
Names: Irujo Ametzaga, Xabier, editor.
Title: World improvised verse / edited by Xabier Irujo.
Description: Reno, Nevada : Center for Basque Studies Press, University of
    Nevada, Reno, [2017] | Series: Conference papers series ; no. 14 |
    Includes bibliographical references.
Identifiers: LCCN 2018037356 | ISBN 9781935709930 (paperback)
Subjects: LCSH: Folk poetry. | Improvisation (Music)
Classification: LCC PN1341 .W74 2017 | DDC 808.1--dc23 LC
record available at https://na01.safelinks.protection.outlook.
com/?url=https%3A%2F%2Flccn.loc.gov%2F2018037356&-
data=01%7C01%7Cdmontero%40unr.edu%7Cde1a3f7bf-
7c9415ae27008d61f0a74cd%7C523b4bfc0ebd4c03b2b96f6a17f
d31d8%7C1&sdata=afvJbzjlqahOWQmfrb70MMftWHBI-
W5oU%2FwJs9mxV4cA%3D&reserved=0

Contents

Improvised Songs of the World

Knowing the person next to you is a beautiful way of getting to know yourself. People who train in *bertsolaritza* (improvised verse singing) learn that lesson from an early age, because it is in talking to the person next to you, in the dialectical process with that person, that you define your own discourse and self-image. The sparks generated off that friction have kept *bertsolaritza* alive for successive generations in the Basque Country. Here in old Europe, in the shores of this particular corner of the Cantabrian Sea, we've been singing to the reality around us century after century.

Slowly, however, we looked up and realized that we were not the only ones. That, throughout the world, there were other languages, other sounds and other bodies improvising and singing verses too. And, with creativity as our guiding principle—those sparks borne off the dialogue between our improvised song and its neighbours—the relationship between us has only grown stronger. It was in the 90s that we started travelling out of the Basque Country and, also, inviting improvised verse singers, experts and researchers from other countries to visit us. In 2015, however, we decided to go a step further in the Mintzola Ahozko Lantegia (Mintzola Oral Literature Workshop), hoisted by the success of Donostia 2016 European Capital of Culture: we set a triple initiative in motion. In the Autumn of 2015 we organized a series of encounters in Leon and the Catalan territories with improvised verse singers from the Catalan territories, Galicia and the Canary Islands; in the spring of 2016 we organized special sessions in the three administrative territories that constitute the Basque Country (the Northern Basque Country in France, and the Basque Autonomous Community and Navarre in Spain), inviting over improvised singers who, like us, perform in minority languages such as Kurdish, Sardinian and Catalan; and, finally, in the summer of 2016, we organized a series of conferences in Donostia. The conferences hosted two types of content: in the evenings we organized artistic sessions with improvised verse singers from Mexico, Wales, Cuba, the Balearic Islands, the Catalan territories and Cyprus, as well as the Basque Country. In the mornings, on the other hand, we organized academic sessions with experts and researchers from all over the world. The articles included in this book are the product of those morning sessions, which, in accordance with the themes of the conference, can be divided into five sections:

It is a uniquely human characteristic to endeavour to make poetry out of oral expression, to play around with the meaning of words, to pay attention to the shadows words cast. It is natural for humans to attempt to make sparks with our spoken endeavours—in any language. Taking that essential aspect of our nature as a starting point, Ruth Finnegan offers us her ideas about the subject of oral poetry.

When Basque improvised verse singers started developing relationships with other improvised verse singers of the world, we realized that we were part of an ecosystem, and that there were invisible threads that bound improvisers from Mexico, Kurdistan, Brazil and the Basque Country together, because we all shared three characteristics: what we do is oral, improvised and expressed through song. It is truly incredible how humans, in so many disparate places of the world, have come to contemplate reality in this same oral, improvised way, through song. Although, of course, each culture has shaped that core idea in a particular way, established a particular relationship with its audience, defined a set of social functions and developed a particular range of characteristics. In the second section of this book, and dealing with the specific shape each of this forms takes in the context of their common ecosystem, Thierry Rougier, Josep Vicent Frechina, Eurig Salisbury and Patricia Tápanes offer a range of descriptive analyses of the improvised songs of Brazil, the Catalan territories, Wales and Cuba.

Besides the common ecosystem the improvised songs of the world share, each improvised song system maintains its own specific ecosystem. *Bertsolaritza*, for example, is contained in the ecosystem of cultural production created in Basque and orally. In other words: the future of *Bertsolaritza* is inextricably bound to the future of the Basque language, *euskara*, and, at the same time, *bertsolaritza* can be said to be an influence in the preservation of *euskara*. This relationship between improvised song and minority language isn't unique to the Basque Country—and when I say minority I am not referring to the size of the language, but to the status of languages that cannot realize their full potential because of their context and historic conflicts. Miren Artetxe and Albert Casals deal with this subject in their articles.

Bertsolaritza has come a long way, both in the creative sense and in the organizational sense, by finding a way of putting artists and influencers on the same path. Our existing projects for research, promotion and transmission stem from that collaboration, and from the Documentation Centre that feeds such projects. All these projects require a good foundation and, at the same time, for the artists and movements involved in the creation of Basque oral culture to maintain an ability to build bridges and reinforce each others' projects, so that each discipline can create a lively and self-sustainable movement in turn and, together, influence society and strengthen, enrich and breathe new life to the Basque oral tradition. One of the main purposes of Mintzola Ahozko Lantegia is to have an influence in these ecosystems.

Improvised song requires an audience; in Basque we say *plazakoa da*, it belongs in the town square. And the square is public: a social, political, economic and cultural context. To research *bertsolaritza*, therefore, doesn't just imply to research cultural production: in researching cultural production, researchers must perforce research its context. *Bertsolaritza* is a door to understanding Basque culture and the Basque Country, to the extent that each improvised song is an opportunity to understand the context in which it takes place. It could be said that *bertsolaritza* holds a miniature mirror to the Basque Country of the twenty-first century, and that, with the turn of the century, new approaches and perspectives have materialized in our midst. The gender perspective is, perhaps, what has caused the greatest shakeup in improvised verse making in the last few years, and Jone Miren Hernandez investigates this in her article.

Bertsolaritza is a self-sustaining movement these days: there is a cohesive, powerful movement around the creation and the support of improvised verse-making that organizes improvised verse singing sessions and hosts a dynamic network of improvised verse schools in villages—which, among other things, are essential for transmission. In 1987 the Bertsozale Elkartea (the Association of Improvised Verse Singing Aficionados) was created with the objective of preserving *bertsolaritza* and strengthening and energizing this farreaching movement and, nowadays, it is a strong structure made up of volunteers and unpaid workers that work to maintain and promote research, transmission and preservation. And there is also the Xenpelar Documentation Centre, which was gifted to *bertsolaritza*. This wide-ranging movement breathes new life into the *bertsolaritza* ecosystem generation after generation. And, in the last section of this book, Xabier Aierdi, Harkaitz Zubiri and Alfredo Retortillo investigate this process of regeneration of the ecosystem from the perspective of *bertsolaritza*'s example.

Artists who travel the world's squares and the organized movements around them have to reflect on many aspects along their journeys. And it is always wonderful to share those reflections with others around us, because the first essential step in this improvised oral tradition is to listen to what the person next to you has just sung, because your response is going to evolve from that. Since we first looked up and started meeting up with improvised verse singers from outside the Basque Country, we've had news of more than one hundred improvised verse singing events. We've taken experts from other countries as travelling companions in this journey and have been able to place most of them on the Map of Cultures we are completing at the newly restored Xenpelar Documentation Centre. Obviously, words are changeable and adaptable work tools and, since the improvised sung verse tradition has words at its core and is also changeable, we're going to have to continuously feed and change that map. And in that continuous process of change, we shall come to know ourselves by getting to know the people next to us.

1

What Is Oral about Poetry?

Ruth Finnegan

To tackle this we need, obviously, to look to two aspects: "poetry" and "the oral," which I will discuss in turn while at the same time unable to avoid a certain amount of overlap as I do so.

So let us then start from the question of "what is poetry?"—not as simple as we might think.

Is *this*?

> I long for you, as one
> Whose dhow in summer winds
> Is blown adrift and lost,
> Longs for land, and finds—
> Again the compass tells—
> A grey and empty sea.

Surely yes, this is a poem.

Yet it was not a set of words written and designed for readers or learnt in school. It was made up by an illiterate Somali lorry driver, then sung in scruffy town taverns, or listened to with half-attention on the radios carried by camel riders across remote

African deserts. It is an example of the Somali genre called *balwo*,[1] developed by the younger urban population in the mid-twentieth century. They were intense love lyrics characterized by condensed imagery and deep emotion and for a time the rage among young men.

And of course it is not just in Somalia. From many years back Africa has been the home of song. How about the praise song, as stirring as many a biblical psalm, for the great king Mutesa in nineteenth-century Uganda?

> Thy feet are hammers,
> Son of the forest [i.e. like a lion];
> Great is the fear of thee;
> Great is thy wrath;
> Great is thy peace;
> Great is thy power.

(Chadwick and Chadwick 1940, 579)

In twentieth-century Africa too and up to today, in plenty, we find unwritten songs of every kind, long or short, high art or popular, with fixed wording or extemporized, sung, danced or chanted. A lover in Tanzania sings

> My love is soft and tender,
> My love Saada comforts me,
> My love has a voice like a fine instrument of
>   music

(Tracey 1963, 20)

---

1. Described and illustrated in Andrzejewski ([1967] 2013).

While a cheerful love song by a young man in East Africa goes

> All things in nature love one another.
> The lips love the teeth,
> The beard loves the chin,
> And all the little ants go "brrr-r-r-r" together.
>
> (Tracey 1963, 20)

Elsewhere too. From India the Gond lover's

> Looking, looking, my eyes broke open
> I could not say a word and she has gone away
>
> (Hivale and Elvin 1935)

or the Ancient Irish, translated as

> My grief o' the sea
> How the waves of it roll
> For they heave between us
> And the love of my soul
>
> (Hyde 1893, 2)

Are such songs 'poetry'? When I embarked on my *Oral Literature in Africa* away back in the 1960s it was a question I had to face.

The first thing I learnt was that in Africa—oh and everywhere, including at home (I remembered the many songs of my native Ireland that I had not really thought about before—there is great virtue in starting from some "exotic" context where all seems new and noteworthy before returning to study one's own, too familiar, culture) and, of course, in Basque country too, most notably—I learnt that songs can indeed be poems: words musicalised. I should not have been surprised for was this not how poetry began? Do we (that is, students of English literature) not speak of Elizabethan lyrics, first sung, now studied as poetry? Or, perhaps less studied, but sometimes equally lovely, the words of hymns, *Lieder* or pop songs?

So too with African songs. When I listen to the sung words, there I find poetry. And all the better for the combination too, the arts that ancient and mediaeval thinkers so rightly joined together in the concept of *musica*—"sung words." And if this is true of them, as of African literature, so too, surely, of Native American, or Indian, or Maori songs. Or Basque.

Sometimes these oral, unwritten, wordings seem pretty unappealing it is true. At first sight anyway.

Take the opening of a lament in Ghana

> Grandsire Gyima with a slim but generous
> arm . . .

How, well, unpoetic!

But the analysis in Nketia's ground-breaking *Funeral Dirges of the Akan* shows how each word had poetic associations and imagery. They give the whole an intense, emotional, metaphorical depth. I suspect that someone unacquainted with English literature would similarly find little poetic in Shakespeare's opening, full of "ordinary" words:

> Like as the waves make towards the pebbled
> shore

> So do our minutes hasten towards their
> end . . .

Or, perhaps my own (and others') favourite Shakespeare sonnet,

> Shall I compare thee to a summer's day?
> Thou art more lovely and more temperate.

For us, each word and its associations (I need not spell them out I think) has poetic weight, it is even more so when they are brought together in a metric line. Is that depth of culturally-transmitted overtone too not a characteristic of poetry? And in Ghana—or anywhere—as in Europe?

And the *sound*. When I look at—or rather listen to—the poems I encounter, whether in full collections, anthologies, gravestones or even written up on the walls of toilets, or inside the carriages of London underground trains—I have to read them aloud, at least in my mind, before I can really *feel* them as poetry. Are you not the same?

Their sound is so lovely. It is not just the metre or the rhyme ("end assonance"), though those are often an important feature of the words that make them not just any old words. It is also the resonances ad assonances within and between lines, flowing through and bringing sound and sense into the heart.

We surely demand of poetry that it should have something of this depth, of emotion, sound and sense, qualities that draw us somehow into the eternal, the universal. William Blake put it so perfectly—"to see the world in a grain of sand. . . ." We find this in Africa too, and literature, written or unwritten, past or present, throughout the world.

There is something about imagery too. Written or unwritten the metaphorical depth of poetry takes us beyond the here and now into a universality of understanding—perhaps of a challenge of understanding, to, again, Blake's "world in a grain of sand." Such imagery, mark you, such meaning can indeed be expressed in writing—but it does not *depend* on writing. It is as clear in oral verbal creations as in the formulations by and for the literate.

Poetry too is surely characterized by a kind of intensity, a densely wrought and felt clustered node of emotion. Hard to define, for it somehow involves all our feelings and in a way has to be learnt and internalized, often only *semi*-consciously, alongside other aspects of the culture—and indeed of the life of the heart. It is conveyed, must be conveyed, with the greatest immediacy by—again, *sound,* often though not always musically marked too, as in hymns and other sung lyrics. Let me recall too the great oratorios of the west that so miraculously combine word, tune, and rhythm in their performances. Like other true poetry they must be performed to *live.* Few are equipped to grasp their full meaning from the score alone any more than the silent reader of a printed verse can grasp its import and, so deep too, its ambiguities. (Think of the poems and poetic passages that have meant the most to you—can you really fully feel them without at least some acoustic resonance?).

Repetition too—the mark of music and its overlapping art of poetry. It can be repeated words or lines, at least in their sound, their rhythm their echoic resonances; of rhyme; of parallelism or alliteration. Repetition, that is, of structure or of sound. Think of the parallelism (repeated but slightly altered echoing and balance) so evident in the poetic passages of the Bible

> A day of darkness and of gloominess.
> A day of clouds and of thick darkness,
>
> > (*The Bible*, Joel 2.2)

Or the alliteration (consonant repetition—which of course has to be *sounded* if, like most other features of poetry, it is to work) well conveyed in Michael Alexander's alliterating translation of the picture of the oral poet in the Old English poem of *Beowulf*, one that needs to be read aloud, that is orally, for its full poetic impact

> Whose **t**ongue **g**ave **g**old to the language
> Of the **t**reasured **r**epertory, **wr**ought a new
> > lay
> **M**ade in the **m**easure. The **m**an's structure
> > **f**ound the **phr**ase,
> **Fr**amed **r**ightly the deed of Beowulf
>
> > (Alexander 1966, 18)

So—music, sound, sense, imagery, sonic and poetic associations, emotional intensity, repetition, a sense of universality behind often quite ordinary words: a path for living (after all what are poems but a mere collocation of words, words made deep and rich as they are breathed and heard in artistry?). All these things, for me, together make up what I would call a poem. Ultimately, though, none of that is enough. It does not need me to tell you that whether in Spain, Africa or Elizabethan England a poem can only live in the breathing of the individual soul, the reader, above all the listener.

So, with these features, words, whether written or not, extemporized or fixed, can be poetry—if we will but listen. For—and here is the point—it must be clear that none of this *depends* on writing. A poem can live—in a sense *must* live—in its sonic qualities, its performance: in short, its orality.

I learnt another lessons too from *Oral Literature in Africa* and also, in a more immediate way, close to home, in constructing my *Poems from Black Inked Pearl* (please excuse me using my own work: it is what I know it the best, also it so well illustrates the issues I want to draw your attention to). What is "poetry" and what "prose"?

This posed a startling challenge. Surely extracting the poems that studded my novel and setting them in separate publications should be easy! They were the bits characterized in the printed novel by jagged right-hand edges as against the justified even print of the main story. But I already knew from my work both on *Oral Literature in Africa* and, more directly, from *Oral Poetry*, that the western convention for presenting poems in print is just that—a *convention*, and a limited culture-specific one too, one that understandably merely takes advantage of the available technology (print) but with nothing universal about it. In other writing schemes (the Chinese of

Mayan for example, or the systems of ancient Greece or Egypt) poems are presented differently. Even in our own the same poem can—and often has been—equally be set with long lines or broken up as shorter with or without stanza divisions, even without lines at all so they look like—well, like prose.

I knew from my comparative reading about oral forms in Africa, Native America and the South Pacific that in that context the distinction between "prose" and "verse" is a slim one—a continuum rather than a clear division, and that (so well pointed out by Dell Hymes 1970) many texts presented as prose could equally, or better, be set as verse. Indeed when I re-read my novel again in what I now know is its full form, that is, *aloud*—or similarly with other examples of what has been regarded as "poetic prose" (think of James Joyce or Walt Whitman or Dylan Thomas for instance, or the sonorous biblical "prose" of John Bunyan's *Pilgrim's Progress*)—it often sounds like poetry. Somehow, as with many African stories, it has an inherent rhythm and resonance about it, feeling almost like a kind of blank verse throughout.

So, depending how you define "poetry," the printed format(s) you first encounter can be a rough initial guide but by no means an infallible one to hat you might want to count poetry. Indeed now that I re-read the novel, especially when I read it in its true medium, that is, aloud, I find that it is *all* in a way poetic in the senses indicated above, a point made in several of its many reviews. I wrote it the way it was given to me (from my unconscious? written by another hand, perhaps a century, a millennium ago?

Who knows?) and it has turned out to be in a kind of blank verse where sound seems in a way as important as sense.[2]

Further, when I sent my manuscript to New York for my lovely Garn Press publishers, I found that I had sometimes hesitated as to how my words should be set: as "prose" or as "verse"? In fact I must tell you that at the last minute I changed some of what I thought of as poems into a "prose" setting, thinking that too much verse-like text might be off-putting. The publishers, after thinking about it, changed them back! I in turn changed some of the Homeric-type similes in the novel—intense, emotional, above all deeply metaphorical—from the prose format in the novel into poetic form for *Poems from Black Inked Pearl*. This verse-prose continuum is apparent above all in oral, unwritten, words. But it is visible too through the fixed-like format of modern print.

Because of this prose-verse continuum[3] I make no apology for also including other passages in the poetry collection that were not, in the original novel, set as verse. This applies particularly to the similes I have just mentioned which, like the overt poems, mark intensified points in the narrative. Some are Homer's own in the sense of being taken from one or other of the translations of those great epics the *Iliad* and the *Odyssey*. Others are my own creation.

---

2. I would, for this reason, like one day to read *Black Inked Pearl* in oral form, that is, as an audio book, perhaps, in the way of many oral poets, embroider and vary a little as I go.
3. Elaborated further in Finnegan (1992).

Or rather—I believe that Homer delivered many different versions with subtly differing wording on the many occasions of his performances and we only have the text of one or at most two of these. These are the beautiful, insightful, similes that he *might* have delivered. I wonder sometimes whether in some sense he actually did and somehow wished them to be captured and disseminated in later centuries. If so, here at last they are within the covers of the *Black Inked Pearl*.

Let me now return to the question of what is *oral* about poetry? Or rather, let me start from the (possibly) rather simpler "*How* is poetry oral?"

So far I have laid the main stress on the *sonic* quality of oral poetry (central in oral stories too incidentally, the main theme of my study of Limba story-telling (Finnegan 1967)). This is indeed a central feature, something that scholars of the past were understandably less aware of but that now, with audio recording, we can capture and analyze, so that now the sonic features of oral poetry shout out at us. This is right. But it is worth remembering too that performance is also *multi*-sensory. Sight (especially in gestures and kinesics generally, but also through costume, accouterments, settings), *many* dimensions of sound (not just voice, fundamental as that often is, and not just volume or dynamics), proxemics, sometimes too fragrance, touch, atmosphere.

Above all we need to recall the role of audiences and their active participation and expectations. Indeed it is the audience, not just the poet, who know, and recognize with, yes, once-again-renewed delight, the familiar themes and settings, and who know well—even, at times, joyously welcome the subversion of—the anticipated space (more, or less) for the beauties of stability, of fluidity or of extemporization. Even if below the level of explicit consciousness, listeners are likely to be fully aware of, and expectant of, the generic conventions: of the expected forms of repetition (in true poetry there is always, I think, an element of this), of the anticipated rhyme scheme—wait for it …—of the ending clausulae, of the stanzaic structure, the intellectual twist or paradox at the end, and in some cases the music. Think of the wonderful extemporized *decima* genre where both singer and hearers feel the anticipations almost in their bodies. And the famous Basque extemporized poetry about which I have often heard my dear friend John Miles Foley talking so enthusiastically, I won't venture to try to present any, but sit back for a moment those of you who know. I think you will be hearing them in your bodies, your ears. Once we have experienced it, the echoic resonances of poetry remains with us.

So much for the oral qualities of unwritten poetry. But, our final question, starting from the other end, can written poetry be "oral"? and if so in what sense(s)?

I think I can be brief, for once we think it through the answer is obvious. Among other things it is well demonstrated in the ancient and mediaeval worlds where, as was the norm for publication and dissemination, "publication" essentially meant reading the manuscript aloud to an audience. Now it may be not just in (silent) print form but in the popularity of broadcasts and audio books, in "the film of the book," and in internet blogs and video trailers (all of these sometimes, as I have found myself, as moving and meaningful as the printed texts themselves).[4] So too in the many poetry-reading and—recital groups with their thronged audiences that in the past years (but maybe long before too) have sprung up throughout the world, or the prolific competitions in the oral delivery of well known (written) poetry in both schools and the adult world. Then there is the Victorian tradition, by no means totally absent in the world today, of couples reading aloud to each other at bedtime, and, everywhere, parents and teachers introducing children to the joys of poetry through their aloud-reading of nursery and other rhymes, and playground children enjoying the beauties of songs, chants and rhymes, captured in writing indeed (Opie and Opie 2001) but in their composition and dissemination fully oral.

Let us however tackle the oral-ness of written forms more directly by returning to our beautiful Shakespeare poems. What about that most lovely and unfading of love poems:

> Shall I compare thee to a summer's day?
> Thou art more lovely and more temperate.
> Rough winds do shake the darling buds of
>   May,
> And summer's lease hath all too short a date.

---

4. https://m.youtube.com/watch?v=JxYo2bKbmJw   ;
https://m.youtube.com/watch?v=BtTqN-62PhE

Sometime too hot the eye of heaven shines,
And often is his gold complexion dimmed;
And every fair from fair sometime declines,
By chance, or nature's changing course,
    untrimmed;
But thy eternal summer shall not fade,
Nor lose possession of that fair thou ow'st,
Nor shall death brag thou wand'rest in his
    shade,
When in eternal lines to Time thou grow'st.
So long as men can breathe, or eyes can see,
So long lives this, and this gives life to thee.

              (Shakespeare Sonnet 18)

Can we grasp the full feeling, even the full meaning, of that poem without *hearing* its rhythm, its assonance, its rhyme system that we know through our ears and anticipate as it comes full circle? In short, its *sound?* Yes, the typographic convention that we see has its message too—telling us among other things that we must think of this bit of text as a poem, *hear* it as such. Some poets too have entranced us with visual effects. I think for example of George Herbert's famous "Easter Wings" where the visible form reflects and intensifies the meaning:[5]

Lord, who createdst man in wealth and store,
Though foolishly he lost the same,
Decaying more and more,
Till he became

---

5. For further examples of visual poetry see Finnegan (2013, chapter 9).

Most poore:
With thee
O let me rise
As larks, harmoniously,
And sing this day thy victories:
Then shall the fall further the flight in me.

My tender age in sorrow did beginne
And still with sicknesses and shame.
Thou didst so punish sinne,
That I became
Most thinne.
With thee
Let me combine,
And feel thy victorie:
For, if I imp my wing on thine,
Affliction shall advance the flight in me.

(Herbert, *The English Poems*, 'Easter wings')

But even here sound surely remains the key and universal poetic element.

I recall too the sonnet from which I took the title of my novel, *Black Inked* Pear (the final line):

Since brass, nor stone, nor earth, nor
        boundless sea,
But sad mortality o'er-sways their power,
How with this rage shall beauty hold a plea,
Whose action is no stronger than a flower?
O, how shall summer's honey breath hold
        out
Against the wreckful siege of battering days,
When rocks impregnable are not so stout,

Nor gates of steel so strong, but Time decays?
O fearful meditation! where, alack,
Shall Time's best jewel from Time's chest lie
          hid?
Or what strong hand can hold his swift foot
          back?
Or who his spoil of beauty can forbid?
O, none, unless this miracle have might,
That in black ink my love may still shine
          bright.

(Shakespeare Sonnet 65)

Neither in the novel where it forms the opening epigraph nor in this (written) paper can I convey this poem—it must be read and heard *aloud*. The heavy sonorous beat of the opening line, conveying so well the claim of permanence, the familiar and beautiful structure and rhyme scheme when you wait for each rhythmic beat and line end that, when they come, sound so inevitable and right; and the battering blunt sound of the "wreckful siege of battering days" and strong "gates of steel." Not apparent at first but beating through any effective reading are, too, the thrusting labiovelar 'b' sounds or the stirring 'r's of the octet—not rhyme exactly but vividly conveying that assonant oral feel. Even the twist in the final couplet with its shimmering sound system needs the pause, the silence, the surprise in the reader's voice to give it its full miracle as we feel, see, hear, almost touch the light-ful eternity of the black ink print and the never to be extinguished "brightness" of that love—so enduring that it touches even the novel that has taken its name.

We have no doubt all encountered these and many many other poems—in Spanish and Italian and Latin too of course—in *written* form. But as with poetry called oral do not they too need their *aloud* delivery? Can you really read them I all seriousness without to at least some degree *hearing* them? And does not poetry that has unquestionably come to us through the written word—think of the Bible with its *Psalms*, its poetic prose—grow and reach its full import—and only then, when read aloud? Are they too not also sonic, resonant, auditory products?

Poetry is indeed oral. It must be.

Enough said.

References

Alexander, Michael, trans. and ed. 1966. *The Earliest English Poems.* Harmondsworth: Penguin.

Andrzejewski, Bronislav W. 2013. "The Art of the Miniature in Somali Poetry." *African Languages Review* 6 (1967): 5–16. Reprinted in B. W. Andrzejewski, *In Praise of Somali Literature.* Milton Keynes: Callender Press.

Chadwick, H. Munro, and N. Kershaw Chadwick, eds. 1940. *The Growth of Literature.* Vol. 3. Cambridge: Cambridge University Press.

Finnegan, Ruth. 1967. *Limba Stores and Story-Telling.* Oxford: Oxford University Press.

———., ed. 1978. *The Penguin Book of Oral Poetry.* Harmondsworth: Penguin.

———. 2012. *Oral Literature in Africa.* 2nd ed. Open Book.

————. 2013. *Communicating: The Multiple Modes of Human Communication.* 2nd ed. London: Routledge.

————. 2015. *Black Inked Pearl, A Girl's Quest.* New York: Garn Press.

————. 2016. *Poems from 'Black Inked Pearl'.* Milton Keynes: Callender Press.

Herbet, George, *The English Poems* [any edition].

Hivale, Shamrao, and Verrier Elvin. 1935. *Songs of the Forest: The Folk Poetry of the Gonds.* London: Allen and Unwin.

Hyde, Douglas. 1893. *Love Songs of Connacht.* Dublin: Gill and Son.

Hymes, Dell. 1970. "Tonkawa Poetics." In *Native American Discourse: Poetics and Rhetoric,* edited by Joel Sherzer and Anthony C. Woodbury. Cambridge: Cambridge University Press.

Nketia, J. H. Kwabena. 1955. *Funeral Dirges of the Akan People.* London: Achimota Publishers.

Opie, Iona, and Peter Opie. 2001. *The Lore and Language of Schoolchildren.* Oxford: Oxford University Press.

Shakespeare, William. *Sonnets* [any edition].

Tracey, Hugh. 1963. "Behind the Lyrics." *African Music* 3, no. 2: 17–22.

2

The Songs Improvised by the Poets of the Brazilian Northeast: Tradition, Urbanization, Expansion, and Animation of a Territory

Thierry Rougier

As a musician and an ethnologist, I teach at the University of Bordeaux. With a particular interest in Latin America, in 1992 I started to research the popular singers who improvise their songs. That took me to the land of Nordeste, the northeastern region of Brazil. There, I found amateurs involved in improvised poetry: the *cantadores* and their admirers, gathered in nocturnal sessions called *cantorias*.

The passion for the spoken word expressed in accordance with the rules of art is a cultural element shared throughout Latin America. Singing poetry and tournaments among poets are widely appreciated. But in Nordeste, people give supreme importance to the total improvisation of sung verses. That is the art of the *repente* (meaning "sudden"), a local

The chapter is based on an ethnomusicological survey conducted in Brazil by the association CORDAE (Centre Occitan de Recherche, de Documentation et d'Animation Ethnographiques), BP 40, 23 Grand rue de l'Horloge, 81170 Cordes-sur-ciel, France. Tel: (33) 05 56 62 19 17; email: talvera@talvera.org; website: www.talvera.org; director: Daniel Loddo.

tradition whose vivacity is remarkable. And today, its actors are much more numerous than ever before.

They are called *repentistas, cantadores,* or *violeiros*: *repentistas,* because they always renew their verses; *cantadores,* because they are popular artists capable of singing any subject proposed by the public; *violeiros,* because they play a *viola,* a kind of guitar emblematic of their profession.

Urbanization boosted the evolution of the *repente* tradition, which originally appeared in the nineteenth century in Sertão, a semi-arid rural area of inland Nordeste. Droughts caused periodic exoduses from this region and Nordestinos constituted the main contingent of migrant workers throughout Brazil. For the last half century, they have participated in the industrialization and the construction of large cities. This rural exodus has depopulated the Sertão, whose itinerant poets of old were transformed into emigrant poets, following their public toward the cities and adapting their art to the modernity.

Urbanization requires social adjustment and cultural adaptation. In the following chapter, I will explain the tradition of the *repente,* the art of the word, whose ethics is spontaneity and adaptation; I will then go on to show how improvising poets have conquered new production spaces, diversifying their activities; and finally, I will discuss the reason for the development of a popular expression in cities where cultural diversity and the pressure of modernity are real-life: the improvisers practice a form of animation combining creation and mediation.

Improvisation: A Mobile Tradition

The emergence of improvised verse is stimulated by the encounter between poets and admirers in a night session. A protocol rules traditional singing: two singers play the *viola,* sitting side by side at the foot of some wall, in front of an audience that often asks them for themes or styles. The poems are always produced by two authors alternating the verses. The poetic dialogue, its emulation, and some rules (for example the obligation to retake in the first line the rhyme that the other has left at the end of his verse, a rhyme that cannot be predicted), everything guarantees the authenticity of improvisation. It is the essential value, before any other formal criteria. In this way, the *repentistas* are distinguished from the other Nordeste poets, the *coquistas.* The latter play a *pandeiro* or drum and usually put together a stanza mixing memorized elements and improvised passages. In addition to this genre, known as *coco de embolada,* there are other genres of oral poetry that are more local, such as: the *coco de roda,* which combines dance, percussion, a choir, and poetry in the coastal zones; the *maracatu rural,* from Nazaré da Mata in the State of Pernambuco, in which improvised verses alternate with very fast music; and the *aboio,* linked to the breeding of cattle, whose poets sing without accompaniment, and which has some Arab or Turkish influence. Compared to these very varied genres, the *repente* is reputed to carry the highest degree of poetic improvisation. I will now characterize its music.

The Music

Unlike the verses, the melody that sustains them is not improvised. The singers learn many traditional tunes by ear, and they use one of these when singing, with some personal variation. Thus, the melodies evolve gradually. New tunes are also created by derivation from the old ones. The poet who opens the song chooses from this vast repertoire the air that seems most convenient to sustain the theme to be developed. The poet who responds to him must repeat this air, demonstrating a particular feeling. This is the constant base of the poem. Certain tunes are always associated with a peculiar poetic form, including a certain refrain. Sometimes, the singer outlines the chosen tune by preluding it on his *viola*.

The melodies are composed in order to sing a note per syllable, except the last one that can be decorated with vibrato or melisma. They are functional and designed to be sung in a metrical poetry in which the lines measure 7, 10, or 11 syllables. The minor mode is exceptional in melodies that have a strong modal character. The most frequent modes are our major scale and alterations of this (the fourth degree of the scale can be pitched a half up, or the seventh pitched a half down, or a combination of both). The notes are often not sung in a temperate way. That means there is a slight difference of tone between the sung and the corresponding note in the playing of the *viola*, divided into twelve equal halves as in a guitar. That is more noticeable when the singer comes from a rural area, since urbanization tends to normalize the modes. Whatever the case, the modes are very variable, but the structure remains the same: the tunes have to be a good support for the poetic forms, which also suffer constant evolution.

The viola playing is the indispensable element to improvisation: the *repentistas* say that their inspiration cannot do without the sound of the strings. They carefully tune the two instruments, which have between 7 and 10 metal strings, some double or triple, grouped into 5 choirs. However, with the exception of some prelude or counterpoint, the *viola* music is extremely monotonous. The whole session is accompanied by the strumming of fingers on a single major chord, barely adorned with any other notes. The constant character of harmony and rhythm is the unifying element; it allows the creation of the unpredictable by the improviser. At the same time, he has to memorize some of what his colleague has said, and think about what he is going to say in the next stanza, put together in a few seconds. The instrument is the poet's tool in the performance, because its music reconciles attention and concentration.

To illustrate that, I will talk about the songs that are not improvised and that mark a pause in the protocol of the improvisation session. At some point, a listener may request a composed song, which is usually nostalgic. It will be interpreted by one of the poets who will then be accompanied with diverse harmonies, as well as major and minors chords (three to six chords for an ordinary song). In short: for a well-known song, the versatility of chords; for the suspense of the poetic tournament, the monolithic character of harmony.

The musical aspects are important for the listeners, who have their preferences according to the vocal, rhythmic, or scenic characteristics of the singer. However, for a singer, these aspects are not criteria determining his professional quality, which depends only on his mastery of poetry and language. Regarding the language, it is the Portuguese in use in Brazil, with high demands on the richness of vocabulary and the sound quality of the rhymes. Poets sing according to the pronunciation of their region of origin and can integrate regionalisms that are often indigenous words. But I am not aware of any improviser producing poetry in any indigenous language of Brazil. Now we must talk about poetry.

The Poetry

The singers perform their oral performances following what they call modalities. That is the structure that links text to music. They have almost fifty different modalities, which are in constant evolution: some fall into disuse, new ones emerge, and they are generally invented in anonymity. The modality determines the metric, the length of the verses, the structure of the rhymes, and sometimes a refrain or a forced melody. The most used modality is the *sextilha*, a six-line verse of seven syllables per line, with a rhyme on the even lines. The *décima* is also widely used and considered a masterpiece in poetic construction. There are two types of *décima*: one has ten lines of seven syllables each line, while the other has ten lines of ten. To build his verse, the improviser has to find four different rhymes and organize them according to a complex structure: ABBAACCDDC. This is what Spaniards call the *décima espinela*, from the name of Vicente Espinel, an Andalusian poet of the sixteenth century. It is still in use in improvised poetry by Chilean, Argentine, and Uruguayan *payadores*, and by Cuban *trovadores*. That means it is a poetic form common to Latin American countries. Here it is worth pointing out an important distinction: when in Spanish they count eight syllables in a line, in Portuguese they count seven because the syllables are counted only until the last stressed one (which is necessarily followed by an unstressed one, or a silence). Likewise, the *decasilábicos* lines of Brazil correspond to the lines of eleven syllables of the Spanish speakers.

The *décima* often ends in a *mote*, a refrain of one or two lines that someone proposes to the two poets before they begin to improvise. One must memorize the *mote* to develop its theme, reuse its rhymes in lines 6, 7, and 8, and repeat it at the end of the verse. Another modality with the same exigency is the *galope*, whose peculiarity is a line of eleven syllables. It is used to sing bucolic themes. Other modalities present different demands, when the two improvisers must alternate the lines instead of the verses. For example, in a modality called *quadrão perguntado*, they must respond in a single line to what was asked in the previous line. In the modalities *o cantador de você* and *gabinete*, manwhile, the singers can show their virtuosity by repeating a long refrain.

The number of forms that can be heard during a *cantoria* session has no equivalent in other genres of oral poetry. To express themselves, poets undergo a demanding tradition that they move forward, inventing new forms, with the goal of excellence. This care for diversification, in addition to an aesthetic particularity, is a test of flexibility for the *cantador*—a thought capable of moving within any frame is also capable of mobilizing in any circumstance. Thus the critical spirit is trained, which is the *cantador*'s ethical requirement.

The Topics

That ethic is revealed by listening to what is sung in the sessions. What is said before the public and how to say it is the major criterion for judging an improvisation. This is termed *oração*, while the other formal criteria are *rima* and *métrica*: a poet has to produce regular lines, without breaking the rhythm; he also has to find many good rhymes. In a session, the listeners propose a subject, suggesting it aloud or by writing it down on a piece of paper deposited on a tray that also collects their contribution. In the same way, a fan of poetry can propose a versified topic that will be the *mote* ending the stanzas. The singers are then obliged to satisfy the requests. They fulfill their role as popular artists by staging the listeners' lives. Each session is an exchange time: ideas circulate and feelings are shared. There is a permanent dialogue between the poets, and between them and their listeners. Thus, the topics are always renewed, through the public in the varied places that singers travel to.

The subject field is very wide. It embraces: the poetic art itself, singing about the value of poets and the grief of those who have left us; fun themes, with the most appreciated being that of a challenge among singers; love, whether happy or unhappy; bucolic subjects; existential or philosophical themes; those that we can term ethical, moralistic, or edifying; and, lastly, social and political issues. A *repentista* must know how to sing about any subject. That is possible by the preparation of improvisers. They refrain from using verses from memory, but learn many words to enrich their imagination. They read books, dictionaries, newspapers, and the Internet, listen to radio and watch television, and especially attend the performances of other *repentistas*. Of necessity, they learn about current social, political, and newsworthy events because they have to comment such matters. They are the scholars of popular culture.

Their knowledge legitimizes their satirical role. At a playful level, they can exchange insults in the *cantoria*, which is a theater of rivalry. From a moral point of view, they have complete freedom of speech to speak about power and denounce its abuses and imperfections, in harsh words. The listeners take advantage of that to propose the most pulsating subjects that the singers will treat with critical spirit. On several occasions I came across the opinion that, "the singers say what the people would say if they could." Many poets consider themselves defenders of the people, at the forefront of social concerns. Many conceive of their art as a popular education movement and *cantorias* as a moment of emancipation of the spirits.

A Conquering Movement: New Production Spaces, New Actors

This description of the *cantoria* was based on a traditional encounter performed *pé de parede* (at the foot of a wall), because they are usually organized in a private house for some party, or in bar or restaurant so as to share the benefits between patron and singers. However, any description would be very incomplete without mentioning new production spaces. Since 1950, contests have been organized by cultural associations in which poets and fans act to promote their art. These events take place in prestigious places of culture such as theatres, welcoming hundreds of people—a larger audience than in family, private, or country sessions. Contests are competitions between duos: two collaborating singers stand on the stage for a thirty-minute presentation, the viola slung over their shoulders, next to a jury that sets the issues and grades the duo, only according to the three criteria of *rima, métrica*, and *oração*. Facing the stage, spectators encourage their favorites. The winners win trophies, cachet, and increased fame in the *repente* community, which is highly competitive. The contests are very successful, with at least one taking place every week in some Brazilian city. Thus, there are frequent opportunities to bring different titles into play. These competitions, invented by the singers, contribute to promoting their art and professionalizing them—nowadays, cachet payment tends to replace the collection on the tray, and contracts are substituted for oral commitments. Tradition evolves in this way, thanks to the rivalry between poets who invent un-precedented circumstances to improvise in.

This occurs on radio programs devoted to improvisation, produced and animated by the poets. During the broadcast, they promote upcoming events and improvise, despite the physical absence of the public, which instead sends in requests by phone or mail. In the areas most affected by the rural exodus, broadcasting is a regular occasion to listen to *repentistas*. Several have learned the basics of their art in this way, before frequenting their first sessions.

Since the late twentieth century and the development of tourism on the coast, beaches are a new space for more humble poets. Without any specific requests, they sing a few stanzas addressing the tourists. They are criticized by their more famous colleagues for walking away from tradition: they sing by day and do not satisfy any specific public demands. In these circumstances, in contrast to traditional sessions, there is little interaction because on the beach they merely beg for money. But what are known as "beach poets" have introduced an unprecedented form of improvisation in new and inauspicious spaces. And in that way, these *poetas de praia* contribute to the expansion and visibility of their practice. It is also worth mentioning recent festivals in public squares, which take place in a context of amplified music and eclectic programming. There, the singers have the opportunity to sing to thousands of people.

Such diversification on the part of the actors typically appears after an opening opportunity. About forty years ago, female poets emerged in an

exclusively male professional environment. The evolution toward the mix of social practices in Brazil
was used by these women to speak up in common.
They equal their male counterparts in terms of artistic ability and critical spirit, and conform to their
vocation as a popular poet commenting on any
topic. But it has not been easy for these women to
emancipate themselves from the reserved attitude
traditionally assigned to them. That may explain the
small number of active women poets today. On the
other hand, the audiences are fully mixed; there are
women passionate about the poetry that accompany
the poets on their tours or do not miss a contest.
However, during my research I have met only two
female poets: they were witness to the difficulty that
exists in overcoming the prejudices, and were proud
of the current evolution.

Record production is an important aspect of the
activity of today's singers, who use their CDs like
a business card to look for contracts. The recorded
material is oral work of a different nature because
it is difficult to improvise in a studio, without any
inspiration stimulated by requests of listeners. This
is, then, not *repente*, but rather an elaborate form of
sung poetry. Instead of writing the poems, the authors repeat them until they reach what they feel is
the best expression. Topics are chosen by the constituted duo and alternate with composite songs. Like
a written published poem, a CD leaves a trail, unlike the evanescence of an authentically improvised
verse. Fans use this medium to hear sung poetry and
compensate for the scarcity of events where they live.

As a result, it is estimated nowadays that there are thousands of these singers and that they far outnumber their predecessors. The dynamism of the tradition accompanies a remarkable qualitative evolution: most *cantadores* of old were illiterate, lived in precarious conditions, and cared little for musical, scenic, or corporate criteria—a fact that does not minimize in any way their quality as great poets whose memory remains alive in the tradition. The epigones work to rise socially, studying, promoting good quality shows, and organizing their profession through associations, hand in hand with other defenders of popular culture.

The activism of the *cantadores* and their admirers, associated in the coproduction of contexts in order to fulfill and perpetuate the *repente,* leads to an appropriation of the spaces in which they take the floor to mobilize consciences.

Mobility, Urbanization, and Expansion: Animation of a Territory

Without stopping, the *cantadores* go to meet new audiences that are also very mobile due to the characteristic emigration of the northeastern region. The climate of the semiarid Sertão, alternating a dry barren season and another favorable to crops, causes seasonal migrations. There are also exoduses due to exceptional droughts. There are other demographic, economic, and political reasons for this exodus: the Nordeste has the worst social indexes in the country, and a negative migration balance compared to all other regions. Groups of Nordestinos have participated in the exploitation of rubber trees in Amazonia, in the industrialization of the south of the country, and in the construction of its capitals, particularly in São Paulo, the largest city in South America. They followed the general patterns of urbanization, a major phenomenon of the last half century: in 1960, when the new futuristic capital Brasilia was built, for one Brazilian living in the city, four were living in the countryside. A few years ago the proportion was reversed. That led to a huge rural exodus in the Sertão, the birthplace of the tradition.

The *cantadores* always moved a lot, on foot or even horseback in the case of the oldest ones that I have interviewed, who were born during World War I. Nowadays, the mobility of the present ones is increasing due to sociodemographic transformations. By necessity, they have followed their public, and for the most part have become urbanized. They have taken advantage of modern means of transport, communication, and information; they have conquered the new spaces of expression already mentioned; raised their educational level and their knowledge of the world; and have had to attend to more diversified requests from listeners confronting the reality of modernity. These new conditions of production have stimulated the *cantadores*, since the capacity to adapt is the source of an improviser's ability.

In a favorable context of rapid transformations, the poets say that they are experiencing a wonderful evolution, being more educated and organized than before. Thousands of poets today live from their popular art within the confines of the vast space of

Brazil, wherever they can magnify the Portuguese language in their poems, and wherever emigrants feel the need to organize a session in which the culture of the northeastern terroir will be sung.

The social dynamics shown by the poets have no equivalent in other genres of oral poetry in Brazil. According to my hypothesis, these genres do not give as much importance to improvisation, that is, its actors reiterate the forms instead of recreating them, and therefore do not encourage the necessary adaptations to the tradition.

In my research I became interested in other categories of popular poets. For example, by way of comparison, the *coquistas* testify that their number is declining, with less and less opportunities to sing. Yet they sing *coco*, a funnier genre than the *repente*, and one characterized by a fast tempo, catchy choruses, and entertaining street shows. In their duels, *coquistas* use a coarse language that is much appreciated and in the *embolada*, they exchange insults. But they improvise only partially, memorizing picaresque verses that skillfully adapt to the context and the reactions of the public. Often, they act as a way of animating open spaces (streets, squares, fairs), which are not conducive to commenting on serious topics. The listeners do not participate in the subject because *coquistas* do not take orders. They deliver little informative or critical content, unlike that heard in *cantorias*.

The two genres share some similarities: in both cases, it is poetry sung in a popular context. But they differ in terms of meaning. When there is more improvisation, a space can be created in which free and profound words can be exchanged. That is typical of the *repentistas*. I have shown that mobility of thinking is related to spatial mobility. It is also related to the desire for social transformation that a *repentista* possesses, wanting to be a spokesman for his Brazilian people.

In conclusion, the songs improvisers animate with represent a territory in which they divulge cultural elements typical of the region in which their art appeared. However, this territory in which today they are updating the tradition is limitless, due to the expansion of the *repente* by following the roads of northeastern emigration. Improvisers are mediators who promote adaptation strategies. They constantly produce and transform the elements of the culture of the people who listen to them.

Bibliography

Loddo, Daniel. 1998. "Cururu e Siriri, chants et musique des fêtes religieuses du Mato Grosso." In *Musiques d'Amérique Latine. Actes du colloque des 19 et 20 octobre 1996 à Cordes (Tarn)*. Cordes: CORDAE/LaTalvera.

Loddo, Daniel, and Thierry Rougier. "Cantadores du Nordeste du Brésil: un art en devenir." In *L'art des chansonniers: actes du colloque de Gaillac des 28, 29, 30 novembre 2003*. Toulouse: Conservatoire Occitan, Centre des Musiques et Danses Traditionnelles Toulouse-Midi-Pyrénées.

Rougier, Thierry. 2006. "Les cantadores, poètes improvisateurs de la cantoria: une tradition en mouvement dans le Nordeste brésilien." PhD diss., University of Bordeaux 2.

Discography

Repentistas nordestinos—troubadours actuels du Nordeste du Brésil. 2006. 2 CDs with an illustrated booklet edited by Daniel Loddo and Thierry Rougier. Cordes: CORDAE / La Talvera.

Payadores de Chile—Poètes improvisateurs du Chili. 2010. 2 CDs with illustrated booklet. Translation of poems and interviews and presentation text by Thierry Rougier. Langon: Daquí, label des Nuits Atypiques.

3

A *Bertso* Home: Architectures of the Word and Constrictions of Gender

Jone M. Hernández García

One would assume there have always been women *bertsolariak*. Why not? They were already noted in the first document making any reference to *bertsolaritza*: a document that mentioned *profazadorak* (to some extent, the forerunners of bertsolariak), the protagonists of a *foru* (charter) established by the Provincial Council of Bizkaia in the fifteenth century, even if it was to ban their occupation. The document describes those women in the following way (Larrañaga 1995, 18): "and about women who are known to be brazen and unruly in their neighborhoods and compose verses and cantos in an inflammatory libelous way."

The reasons for this prohibition are unknown, with only the odd hypothesis in this regard. Thus, Joxe Azurmendi (1990) links both the ban and the progressive disappearance of these women that followed to the Council of Trent (1545–1563). Whether this was an influencing factor or not, it is true that from that moment on women were less involved in bertsolaritza. Whether in the form of some names and surnames, or just names, there only exist traces of women (for example, the *bertso* prompter Irigaineko dama, "the lady of Irigain").[1] On the contrary, in recent decades—during the age of contemporary bertsolaritza—the profiles of numerous women bertsolariak have been much more prominent, as have the difficulties they face when it comes to appearing in public. Specifically, in recent years several of them have reflected on the obstacles they face, and one could already say that we are on the way to establishing an analysis of bertsolaritza undertaken from a gender perspective.

To pinpoint the beginnings of this process at some point, I would locate it in 1995 with the publication of "Emakumeak Plazara" in a monographic edition of the journal *Bertsolari* (no. 17). That edition discussed women bertsolariak in the past, but also women in bertsolaritza in the 1990s and, looking toward the future, the emerging young women bertsolariak. There, too, as well as bertsolariak, women theme-prompters, judges, presenters, bertso session organizers, and researchers were front and center. That monograph revealed a new reality while raising

---

1. Carmen Larrañaga has been a pioneer in her works collecting the names of women bertsolariak. Her trajectory has been reflected in several publications (1994, 1995, 1997). Nowadays, more scholars are following in the footsteps of Larrañaga. The Bertsozale Elkartea (Association of the Friends of Bertsolaritza) gives information about this on one of its webpages: http://www.bertsozale.eus/eu/generoa. There one can find information about women bertsolariak and works about women bertsolariak.

several questions, doubts, and lines of inquiry for the future.

Thereafter, in the years that followed, further reflections, testimonies, and debates emerged, always focusing on women bertsolariak and their reality and experiences.[2] In this regard, and by means of a very brief summary, one could say that the aim of these works has been to examine and reveal the influence that the gender system and gender roles have had and continue to have in bertsolaritza. Linked to that goal one should underscore the fact that the elements and phenomena detected by that analysis are similar to those found in other social models. As one woman bertsolari told me:[3] "In the final analysis, in bertsolaritza you see the same thing as in other social spheres . . . You speak with any woman and, whether a housewife, a bertsolari, or a police officer, we find the same problem . . . or a professor, we come across exactly the same problem." And several people have reported the same situation, some of them academics, but in the main bertsolariak themselves.

Taking those studies and reflections into account, one could say that the analyses have mainly detected the influence of the gender system in the following spheres: (1) in the history of bertsolaritza,

---

2. There is information about this trajectory at the aforementioned website of the Bertsozale Elkartea (http://www. bertsozale.eus/eu/generoa/dokumentazioa), with this section including different materials about bertsolaritza and gender. Moreover, it also includes many interesting references about gender and feminism (accessed July 3, 2016).
3. Interview conducted on December 1, 2009.

in which women are clearly invisible; (2) in the imbalances and reproduction of gender roles between women and men that occur in the transmission of bertsolaritza; (3) in the differences one notes in the professional careers of female and male bertsolariak; (4) in bertso-related initiatives and in the participation of men and women in these; (5) on stage, when creating bertsoak, in the gender inertias, behaviors, or practices that take place; and (6) in general, in the existing prejudices about bertsolaritza in society as a whole as well as among bertsolariak and bertsolaritza aficionados.

It has been said that bertsolaritza is a reflection of society and, inevitably, as in society as a whole, the gender system (that is, according to Raewyn Connell, work, power, and cathexis; see Connell in Del Valle 2002) would be located at the core of its organization. Connell's work demonstrates, with absolute clarity, the deep roots this system possesses as well as just how difficult and even impossible it can be to extract them. With this in mind, it is perhaps rash to think that any achievements made by women bertsolariak are signs of society having achieved equality. Likewise, one could say that such achievements are not sufficient enough to think that equality has at least been reached within the sphere of bertsolaritza. On the contrary, any interpretation and evaluation of those achievements calls for special attention and extreme prudence. Moreover, I would say that time (a historical perspective) is needed in order to be able to see how the current situation will evolve in the future. As noted above, it is worth being absolutely clear about the fact that discussion of women bert-solariak only really began at the outset of the twenty-first century.

Thus, while women bertsolariak make some progress and as long as studies follow up on avenues that have already been opened up, I will be involved in the new opportunities we should be exploring. Although I believe we need to delve further into the approaches, theories, and perspectives that have been advanced to date, it seems to me that the complexity of the contemporary situation obliges us to explore new proposals. That is, precisely, the chief goal of this chapter: namely, without ignoring the new avenues that have been explored, to also examine new theoretical perspectives and approaches, at a time when equality has become more *fluid* than ever, with the aim of exposing the boundaries that still exist nowadays.

The chapter takes into account the bertsolari and the audience in particular, transforming the relationship or link between them into an area of consideration. Starting from that relationship, the focus is also placed on the bertso because that link is reflected in the bertso itself, it being both the context and the outcome of the relationship between transmitter and listener. Lastly, the nature and meaning of the bertsoak and the bertso structures will be examined, because I believe that the main boundaries bertsolaritza has today, from the gender perspective, are to be found *there somewhere*. Therefore, as well as highlighting several key concepts linked to the bertso—for example, ellipsis and

metonymy alongside John Foley's "traditional referentiality" (Foley 1991)—the opportunity they give
one to encourage a feminist interpretation will be
highlighted.

Thereafter, there will be a brief discussion of the
audience and the bertsolari. Then several elements
that are helpful when it comes to representing the
link between the two will be presented. Finally, taking into account these elements, there will be a discussion about the opportunities that emerge from
studying bertsolaritza from a feminist theoretical
perspective. The latter would be a provisional exercise based on the hypotheses that have emerged on
the way to amassing the empirical work.

On the Relationship between the Bertsolari and the Audience

As noted earlier, to date when studying the influence gender has had in bertsolaritza there has been a
special focus on elements linked to the social structure, or the tradition of bertsolaritza, or the way in
which it is carried out. These considerations attach
important nuances to the wide-ranging or general
studies on bertsolaritza: when women bertsolariak
reflect on this, they add a dimension linked to life
experiences to the previously formulated analyses,
but above all that of being a woman has been the
main topic of discussion because in many cases this
has been a reflection of what happens in society as
a whole. From that point of view, what is missing is
an analysis from within the bertso logic itself, starting from the particular nature or idiosyncrasy of the

bertso and the context/situation it creates. Carmen Larrañaga (1994) most successfully approaches this kind of research because her works are primarily focused on the characteristics of bertsolaritza, the bertso, and the bertsolari.

Nevertheless, acknowledging deficiencies does not mean questioning the productive research undertaken to date. Thanks to this work, the introduction and diffusion of the gender perspective is now revealing different previously hidden situations and realities. The Bertsozale Elkartea itself is also being helpful in this regard, through its efforts to promote more equal practices.[4] Just as one hears in several other social spheres, so in bertsolaritza circles too there have been calls to look at the reality from a feminist perspective.

Still, in a society living in the illusion of equality perhaps it is not enough nowadays to adopt a feminist perspective. One would think that for someone who is completely blind such a perspective would not be sufficient to correct the incapacity. In the same vein, and given that we are now considering

---

4. Through different initiatives, in recent years the situation of women, the subject of gender, feminism, and so on have been topics of debate in the field of bertsolaritza. Conferences, lectures, training sessions, and other kinds of activities have been organized in order to publicize the concern of women bertsolariak, and in general, to reflect on equality; in short, to promote equality. Worth mention is the "Gender group," a working group created within the Bertsozale Elkartea itself in 2008. Within this group women and men bertsolaritza aficionados promote the study, debate, and discussion of equality.

vision, it seems appropriate to recall what John Berger observed a few decade ago: "the way we see things is affected by what we know or what we believe" (Berger 1972, 8). More than forty years later, those words continue to be as suggestive as they were at the time and if we look closely at Berger's argument, we realize that we should rethink/redirect the line of inquiry. The implications of that are many and multifaceted, but I would like to highlight two from among all these.

On the one hand, the observation itself is transformed into a subject of examination rather than those that have been typically observed (women and the condition of women): the origins of that observation, its base, and the elements that make up that observation. On the other, and linked to the former, would be the metaphoric example of the work of an underwater diver: because we should better comprehend the base structure, tools, or mechanisms—localized and within each expression—that ensure the reproduction of elements. Applying this problem to bertsolaritza, I would say that two or three principal questions surface: first, from where does the audience *watch/listen*? How and where does the audience *position itself* in the face of the bertsolari's activity? Second, how do the bertso and the bertsolari respond to those foresights? To what extent does the bertso—not just its contents, but also its features, its structures—help (or not) that observation? Finally, there could also be a third important question: where does the bertsolari position her/himself in the face of all this?

So far, although there is just a hypothesis in response to these questions, I would like to explain and extend it in this chapter, even fully aware that the empirical or ethnographic dimensions need to be worked on.

By way of a starting point in this argument, one should say that two perspectives intersect: on the one hand, that of the bertso and the bertsolari; and on the other, that of spectators or the audience. Both are necessary to produce bertsolaritza, therefore in order to understand the hierarchy or lack of parity orchestrated by the gender system we should pay attention to both: we should examine and understand both and, along with that, the logic between both of them; because all those elements take part in the process of making up a bertso session.

The following is clear: a bertso is the glue between the bertsolari and the audience, the link between the two of them, the space in which they come together, a meeting point.

The Bertso as a Communicative Framework

In order to describe what a bertso is, a technical definition can be used: "The bertso consists of a sung, rhymed and measured discourse" (Egaña in Garzia, Sarasua, and Egaña 2001, 83). But when discussing bertsolariza, it is clear that a bertso is much more than that. Different definitions have been and will be made in relation to the bertso that surpass technical areas, but among all of them, I concur with that of Joseba Zulaika, who states that (1988, 213): "making [a] bertso creates a frame in which communication other than ordinary conversation is permitted." Pursuing this idea more deeply, Zulaika (ibid.) says that bertsoak are a useful means of expressing messages that are not or do not usually need to be expressed (because they are "taken as given") in everyday life, in the day-to-day grind (such as "We are Basques," "We all belong to the same country," and so on). Along the same lines, we should add that a bertso creates a special forum or discursive space in order to diffuse messages about what is appropriate in a community. In fact, the linguistic skills of bertsolariak give them legitimacy to address the whole community and to speak about that community's identity. One often hears the comment that the bertsolari is the voice of the people, but the bertsolari is nothing without the bertso.

For that reason it would be interesting to know, within this communication space, forum, or word structure, where does the nature of the bertso, the structure of the bertso, and, in the final analysis, its strength come from? How does the bertso function? These are inescapable questions because, as well as the discourses and arguments articulated by bertsolariak, the structure and form those contents take on are key in order to understand the successful connection they achieve with the community.

The Bertso and Group Identity, Form, and Group Sociology

One of the main reasons for the persuasiveness of Zulaika's view would be the relationship of the logic within the bertso with Basque culture, and especially with its causal connections. As Manuel Lekuona (1978) himself states, in bertsoak threads are created via images. It makes no sense to ask what the relationship is between two images that appear in a bertso. The thread (those images) is to be found in the wording itself. Those images may be images connected to group identity or individual identity; nothing else is needed, not any logical consequences or any political or historical treatise: "'Why' they are related is 'because' they are part of the same strophe" (Zulaika 1988, 209).

Within this logic images are trapped within the structure of the bertso, and melodies and rhymes facilitate their relationship. At that moment a *trope* (metaphor, metonymy, or synecdoche) is created. In this process, too, ellipsis is a fundamental element because it structures the breaks that occur within the discourse. The thread or the argument is constructed through images and it is important, therefore, that those images are precise and visual. Ellipsis establishes a kind of causality. In Zulaika's words (1988, 219), "The expressive power lies precisely in the discontinuity of the images, in their not being linked in a causal process, in the elliptical yet metaphorically successful connection of images belonging to different domains of experience. Causality here is ellipsis."

Ellipsis, then, becomes the essence of the bertso because it is constituted around the bertso itself. In this same vein one could say that in the bertso silence (that which is not said) is as important as the word.

However, one must not forget that on the other side of the bertso there is the audience or the listeners.

How do they receive the bertso? How do they appropriate it? How do they interpret it? We know less about that and in order to complete the studies done to date, it would be necessary to embrace that approach as well.

The Bertso (Word) as a Symbol, Transformed into a Social Link

If there is one point of reference in studies of oral traditions it is John Foley. Thanks to him, different directions in the study of orality have been opened up and expanded in recent decades. One of those would be that involving "receptionalist" perspectives. In this case, a preoccupation with or interest in orality is located in the listening or receiving process, transforming the listener into the protagonist.

Foley attempts to develop in the field of orality the perspective Wolfgang Iser applied to literature (Iser 1978 in Foley 1991). In both cases the main idea is the following: in an oral and a written text the activity would be divided up, with the author, the text, and the listener (or reader) all being participants. Following Iser's ideas, the work of art itself would be located between the *text* (or the oral production) and the readers (or listeners). In this way, a work of art could never be something fixed and nor could the receiver (Foley 1991, 39–40). Both Iser and Foley underscore the active nature of receivers at all times: "we are urged to leave behind the conception of the literary work as object and to recognize our own complicity in bringing artistic 'objects' to life" (Foley 1991, 40). In the same vein, Foley raises the notion of the "implied reader."

This active attitude oversees a special task, namely, filling in the "gaps" that texts or works of art have. As both Foley and Iser say, those gaps should not be conceived as "mistakes." On the contrary, in their opinion they offer a means of cultivating and developing readers' or receivers' imagination (Foley 1991, 41). That, ultimately, would alleviate the text (whether written or oral), increasing its interest. In this approach Foley raises a fundamental nuance: in his opinion, in the field of orality tradition would play an important role in that active attitude on the part of the audience (Foley 1991, 45): "we may say that all members of the audience interpret the text according to a shared body of knowledge that is their inheritance."

Therefore, within this active attitude, by means of tradition—or to use Foley's expression, "traditional referentiality," which would be a key term—previously created texts and "performances" are brought up-to-date, becoming part of the textual or oral production that is on the point of being created: "Traditional referentiality, then, entails the invoking of a context that is enormously larger and more echoic than the text of work itself, that brings the lifeblood of generations of poems and performances to the individual performance or text" (Foley 1991, 7).

Foley emphasizes the importance of the traditional referentiality concept in the oral tradition, highlighting the prominence not just of the text but also of the context in the creative and diffusive process. He speaks about an "unspoken" context that goes beyond the words of the text (Foley 1991). In

Foley's opinion, those elements that remain concealed exist long before any specific oral production (a bertso sung by a bertsolari in a specific event) is created or appears, and it is those that impart a traditional touch to the production. The artist will achieve a more complete piece when they use/insert those elements, because the text, as well as incorporating "superficial" components, also takes into account tradition. As Foley says, in that connection that emerges with those elements beyond the text one can find the support and the method that the oral tradition uses to channel meaning, those that would facilitate the exchange between artist and audience. Foley also terms this "metonymy," the accumulated knowledge and experience gathered by tradition, which constitutes production (the text and so on) (Quick 2011).

As is well-known, in the case of metonymy one piece represents the whole, imparted by tradition and making use of "what is known and what does not appear." I am referring here to the non-material heritage, that which is accumulated in silence, that which is transmitted in silence, and that which remains invisible. The oral tradition, however, draws from that source and reveals what is there, if we know how to hear it. Mikel Azurmendi (1993) also addresses metonymy—that which would take the form of metaphor—in his research on orality, because in his opinion they are necessary elements in the socialization process: "[the everyday bread and butter of any society] are those things that inform in human action, allowing men to become men, women to become women, and for babies, young people, adults, and the elderly to be true model humans" (Azurmendi 1993, 125).

Azurmendi's words are especially interesting because he applies Foley's approach to Basque culture, to Basque orality, and to Basque tradition. They draw attention to metonymy and, in general, the importance of the trope and the word. Not just any word; but the measured word, the direct word, the meaningful word, the word that is the measure of humanity, and, in traditional culture, the word that is the measure of men: as an old Basque proverb states, (Azurmendi 1993, 232), "*idia adarretik, gizona hitzetik*" ([you can catch hold of] an ox by its horns and a man by his words).

For me, the works of Zulaika, Foley, and Azurmendi are central, primarily because they establish—each from the perspective of their own discipline, personal interests, and research methods—a means by which to represent the bertso as a symbolic link between language and society. Within this link three different but related meanings that have thus far been explained can be highlighted. Let us recall them.

First, the bertso establishes a (special) communicative field that facilitates nontypical communication practices. Second, in formal (or technical) terms the bertso has a structure or an architecture that intersects with a sociological group (with a community in the anthropological sense). Third, the bertso is transformed into a symbol insofar as it creates, recreates, and expresses a social link. The word constitutes a group, taking on a magic nature that could be defined as *mana* (Crépeau 1993 in Surrallés 2003, 776).[5]

In sum, this would be the fundamental architecture of bertsolaritza, a home furnished by the word. Yet if we understand the bertso this way, how would we interpret it from the perspective of gender? What influence does the gender system have in the communicative field that the bertso represents? What of that influence in its identity-based nature? And in its symbolic nature?

Architectures of the Word and Constrictions of Gender

As stated, the bertso creates a special field of communication. In Zulaika's opinion, things that are not typical in everyday life, in the routine of day-to-day life—because they are taken as given, as understood—are said in bertsoak. On the other hand, in that field the bertsolari will have the opportunity to speak to the community, to direct her or his messages to the community, to speak about the community, and, often, will also get permission to speak on behalf of the community.

As can be seen, the bertsolari possesses extensive authority and, in practice, is the chief overseer of this space. They will feel a great responsibility as well as tension. Bertsolariak need an audience but, at

---

5. The concept of *mana* is very deep-rooted in the tradition of social anthropology. Briefly, *mana* refers to power, effectiveness, and prestige, but always linked in some way to magic, religion, or beliefs.

the same time, cannot get involved too much in the audience. They are also artists who need to nurture their self in order to facilitate the creative process. This is how one bertsolari put it to me in an interview: "You sing to an audience, you can't escape from that . . . [but I must] connect with myself, with my body, with my emotions, feelings."[6]

The engineering work bertsolaritza demands is made up of three pillars. First: technique (melody, rhyme, and so on); second, discourse or content; and third, being positioned on a stage and in a relationship with an audience: "how you are with your body and your emotions at that moment, on stage . . . and how you manage that."

The topic of preparation and training has often been cited when discussing the differences between girls and boys or women and men who are bertsolariak. While there have been different reflections on this, generally speaking the following ideas are highlighted: on the one hand, when children, adolescents, or young adults go to bertso school,[7] they already bring with them the consequences of receiving different and differentiating socialization processes. The starting point for girls and boys, when it comes to training in and performing bertsolaritza, is different. There have been multiple references to this in recent years. By way of example, Nagore Soroa observes the following (Gaztelumendi 2010):

---

6. Interview conducted on May 6, 2016.
7. A school or academy, normally at the municipal level, in which children, young people, and adults learn how to do bertsolaritza.

Boys, for example, are not too bothered about appearing foolish. They are quite comfortable, most of them, in front of people . . . A boy is almost certain he'll get some applause and he'll take risks. A girl, however, if you appear in front of people, I think, most at least, don't feel very comfortable. They'll feel pressure: "what should I say, what are people expecting of me," and she's not used to that environment, she's not used to starting a bertso and, if she makes a mistake, saying to herself "it doesn't matter," if people laugh at her, "it doesn't matter." She doesn't usually appear in front of people very willingly.

Girls and boys are socialized to embrace different attitudes, behaviors, and tasks in life and that is obvious when they begin moving in the field of bertsolaritza (and to some extent in other kinds of activities that are developed or take place in front of people). Nevertheless, whatever the difficulties, girls—or some girls at least—carry on and enter into a training process. And what happens in that process? We should probably know more about this or in a little more depth but, even though only by way of a hypothesis, I would say that in that engineering work brought on by bertsolaritza, girls and boys can be fairly equal at the technical and discursive level. But another thing altogether is the attitude, preparation, skills, and so on of some as opposed to others when it comes to those obligations, to working the stage, and relating to the audience.

It is no coincidence that, during the current school year (2015–2016), in the newly established empowerment workshops specifically aimed at women, the latter has been the most developed field (appearing on stage, relating to the audience). Predictably. Once again we are speaking about the need to understand more deeply that relationship between audience and bertsolari.

In his aforementioned work, Berger (1972) writes about the prevailing representation of women in the field of fine arts and explains perfectly the role imposed on women by the gender system (power) and the goal of this (assuring women's subordination). Through gender socialization, women—for being women—are trained to look at others (linked to the concern for and looking after others, and other kinds of services); and also to be looked at by others (in this case, above all, as objects, linked to their bodies, beauty, and sexuality); never to speak, to give their opinion, to take their own decisions, and to argue their positions. As Carmen Larrañaga contends, "femininity, or what is exhorted of it, is sustained by negation and absence" (Larrañaga 1994, 42).

Negation and absence, but silence as well. Even more so in bertsolaritza. The bertsolari Maialen Lujanbio addressed this already ten years ago in an interview on Euskal Telebista (the Basque public television channel):[8] "Let's say you're sixteen. A girl,

---

8. The interview appeared in an episode of the bertsolaritza

a woman, who goes out in public. How much confidence does that girl have in her word, in the importance her word may have? What happens if no one's interested in her word? I think we disregard our own word and the value of our word."

Playing with the word, on stage, before an audience, women bertsolariak have called into question the role (invisibility, silence) they were assigned historically by the gender system. And not just that. They are breaking with the norm, but in doing so they are also questioning the identity of the *other*, in this case male identity, for in our society the basic norm and fact of the matter is that there are two genders and two identities, female and male, which define each other in opposition to one another. Larrañaga captures this perfectly (1994, 43):

It is not easy for women to find a warm welcome in bertsolaritza. All the more so not because they break with the norm, as Zulaika suggests—which undoubtedly they do—but because their presence chips away at the cement on which our most solid identity rests. Knowing how to be a man and not a woman, that is the difference that is of prime importance, and that which determines in the male his masculinity, which is cultivated not by [masculinity]

show *Hitzetik Hortzera*, broadcast on May 8, 2005. That episode was titled "Bertsolaritza and women." A transcription of the show—which featured, besides Lujanbio, many other bertsolariak, most of them women—can be found on the website of the Bertsozale Elkartea: http://www.bertsozale.eus/eu/generoa/dokumentazioa/artikuluak/2005-05-08%20Bertsolaritza%20eta%20emakumea%20-%20Hitzetik%20Hortzera.pdf (accessed July 3, 2016).

itself but instead in opposition to femininity, resisting it.

Following the argument of the anthropologist Mary Douglas (1991) we may think that, when bertsolariak comment on or joke about women's femininity in bertso sessions, it is a way of establishing symbolic boundaries in a quest to protect their own masculinity. And through such a strategy women and women bertsolariak are reminded over and over again where their place is: they have been taught to be looked at, not at all to shift the gaze to their inner selves and from there express themselves; they have been raised to nourish others (the people around them, relatives, and so on) emotionally or with emotions, but without being encouraged to be emotional (or at least too emotional).

Women bertsolariak, their bodies, their clothes (miniskirts, heels, and so on) chip away at the order of the masculinized domain. This being the case, in the desire to confirm the symbolic boundaries between masculinity and femininity, sometimes femininity is over-emphasized by playing with simple images, views, or expectations connected to women, in other words with stereotypes. Other times, masculinity, its features, and its obligations will be highlighted, again in the desire to establish firmly its differences with women or femininity.

Following the theory of James Fernandez, Zulaika (2008, 241) says: "in the appropriate cultural context anyone can become a lion, a cow, or an octopus." This is in some way fulfilled in bertsolaritza because as the bertsolari Andoni Egaña observes in

Asier Altuna's 2011 documentary on bertsolaritza, in one bertso session he can be Obama, an old bicycle, an elver fisherman, an Athletic Bilbao soccer player, or a scorned lover. And the audience goes along with it because it is involved with the bertsolari.

Understanding its qualitative and subjective nature, how is it that bertsoak and that nontypical field of communication established by bertsoak cannot erase the dichotomy between women and men?

"If there is no difference, there is no unity," contends Larrañaga (1994, 43). If there are no differences, where is masculinity? Where is femininity? From where do one and the other draw their strength? Larrañaga herself explains that the differences based on sex are unquestionably rooted in our culture. In the eyes of society this would appear undeniable. Another thing is the cracks that feminism and other kinds of critical ideologies have introduced into that firmly held view. Indeed, and especially in recent decades, new arguments and models have been put forward to understand, represent, develop, and create identity, as stated, from the perspective of many different feminist currents and positions.

All of this would lead us to reflect on the role differences play in the process of creating and developing identity, an interesting challenge but one that, for now, must be put to one side.

Whatever the case, turning once more to the issue of identity in bertsolaritza, we should bear in mind—as noted earlier—that Lekuona (1978) and, especially, Zulaika (1988) see a parallel or link between the form (structure) of bertsolaritza and group dynamics/identity. Others, meanwhile, also note this link in similar traditions, rituals, or celebrations in other contexts. Alexandre Surrallés, for example, after examining the views of several experts who work on Amazonia, observes the following: "most earlier and more recent studies agree on the existence of a link between these forms (forms of ceremonial dialogue) and the sociology of the group expressing them" (Surrallés 2003, 776).

In order to apply these ideas to our case, I will return to Zulaika's theory in order to recall that the word needs ellipsis to make up a bertso, because the links and complementariness between them impart it with power and strength. At the same time, recalling the words of Surrallés, one could say that ellipsis—as a syntactic construction of phrases—has a connection to Basque oral culture because it acclaims literalness, the word as commitment, and economy of expression (Zulaika 1988, 230). As stated above, in traditional Basque culture the ideal person is totally linked to the ideology of the word, because in oral culture everything is subject to the authority of the word. The word must be precise, measured, and meaningful. Like people. Like men. Like bertsoak. Women, however, when they come into contact with the word, have no identity. Larrañaga explains this idea in the following terms (1994, 40): "the distance between the genders (male and female) is, therefore, more than distance; because, strictly speaking, the woman does not even exist. Or, in any case, she is that difficult and indefinable hybrid: half adult, half child; an eternally half-made creature, obstinately unfinished."

The word of (Basque) women cannot represent (Basque) culture because it is not precise, measured, and meaningful. But, moreover, the word of women does not lead to action because it is a word linked to the home (and affect), not to the plaza or the outside public world, to competition, to power, to *joko* or the game, in a serious competitive sense (Larrañaga 1994, 43–44). As the Basque expression goes, *Hitza duen gizona, hitzeko gizona* (The man who possesses the word is a man of his word). The word of women is not suitable for action.

On the other hand, the motives included in the bertso are images created by the community. Ellipsis, with the aid of rhyme and melody, binds what seem like loose images, creating the option to insert several previously mentioned notions, especially the concepts of metonymy or traditional referentiality. The audience will use "that which is not said because it is understood" or tradition in order to establish a relationship or fill in the gaps, referring to a very sensitive and subjective field. However, that space, which can be ambiguous and untouchable, is more understandable from feminist theory because it has been the traditional home of women and because in several cases it has been transformed into an area of research. Women bertsolariak also mention that place—even though they do not refer to it as such—every time they set foot onto the stage: they renounce a past, an imposed silence, gender instructions and roles, inertias. Their presence alone, their bodies and voices, question tradition ("traditional referentiality" in Foley's words) and call for it to be deconstructed.

Yet as well as their presence and bodies, they have used the word itself to transform the bertso. It would demand a more thorough and definitive study, without any doubt, but could we not argue that the "narrativity" developed by Maialen Lujanbio in bertsolaritza is a kind of provocation aimed at ellipsis? Although subtly, prudently, and suggestively, Lujanbio offers up connected and linked ideas/images. In this case, ellipsis is not something that would bear out traditions, stereotypes, or "that which is known"; ellipses must be filled in by listeners through reflection, really giving them some thought. Lujanbio's arguments are aimed at every listener, rather than at the wide abstract community, but, and because of that, she is provocative and transgressive. Awkward.

That said, there are other moments and situations in which awkwardness is apparent. As regards that, if there is one mythical scene in the history of bertsolaritza that portrays the most fitting example of such awkwardness, it is that of Fernando Aire or "Xalbador" crying.

Xalbador took part in the 1967 National Bertsolaritza Championship and finished runner-up. However, he was the central figure in that year's championship.[9] In the final stages of that final—during the head-to-head section—Xalbador and Manuel Olaizola or "Uztapide" faced off against each other as

---

9. The details of this story were taken from information published in Wikipedia: https://eu.wikipedia.org/wiki/Xalbador (accessed on June 3, 2016).

they had been the best performers to that point on the day according to the judges. When the decision was made public, boos and whistles from the audience—those who disagreed with the decision to choose him for the final head-to-head section, most likely on account of the fact that they did not fully understand his Northern Basque dialect—filled the Anotea pilota court, where the championship was being held, for a minute and a half, spoiling the atmosphere. Then, as the expressions of disagreement quietened down, a barrage of applause were heard alongside whistles and the general din. The audience was divided in two: when it seemed that the whistles were silencing the applause, fans of Xalbador stood up and applauded their bertsolari. One of the judges asked the bertsolariak to begin the session, but both remained steadfastly silent. Finally, Uztapide, amid all the shouts and howls, performed the presentation bertso.

Then Xalbador's turn arrived. As he was about to begin his turn, a cacophony of whistles and applause were heard once more. In the end, when the voice of the spectators abated, Xalbador performed the following bertso:

> *Anai-arrebok, ez, otoi, pentsa*
> *neu're gustora nagonik,*
> *poz gehiago izango nuen*
> *albotik beha egonik.*
> *Zuek ezpazerate kontentu*
> *errua ez daukat ez nik,*
> *txistuak jo dituzue bainan*
> *maite zaituztet oraindik.*

(Brothers and sisters, please
don't think I'm thrilled,
I'd be happier,
looking on from the sidelines.
If you're not happy,
it's no fault of mine;
you did jeer
but I love you still.)

When he came to sing "If you're not happy, it is no fault of mine," there was an unprecedented round of applause that stopped the bertsolari in mid-bertso for a short while, before he could end it with the last two lines. With that bertso, Xalbador managed to bring the two sides that had formed among the spectators back together. Abandoning his native Lower Navarrese Basque dialect, he adapted the bertso to Gipuzkoan Basque—the dominant dialect among the listeners—and that way he managed to reach into their hearts.

This moment experienced by Xalbador clearly reveals that if bertsolaritza is one thing, it is that fluid link that emerges between audience and bertsolari.[10]

---

10. In order to portray this link I would like to invoke the words of Jorge Oteiza that, I think, capture it better than anyone else (2007, 117): "The bertsolari's technique is that he is front of everyone and disappears into his inner reality. From where his words emerge (and will continue to emerge). I usually say that it is as if he allows himself to be submerged in a river (the river of his internal vision). Now I also say that it is as if he abandons the audience (that is listening to him) on a beach. And he walks backwards toward the sea. And, completely submerged, he speaks to us in that watery rhyme that comes to

The bertso is located there somewhere in between, as a social symbol, as a means of bringing about that social link. It ultimately serves to connect the word, the Basque language, the bertso, and so on.

After studying welcoming ceremonies in Amazonia, Surrallés highlights the importance of the word in such ceremonies; in his opinion, whenever words are exchanged culture emerges, and alongside that social links. This is how he describes that special moment linked to the word (Surrallés 2003, 775): "For in these welcoming ceremonies language plays a crucial role because the culminating moment is the spoken dialogue; the conceptual abstraction of a social link becomes concrete at the very moment when the first words are exchanged."

But as he himself explains, the exchange of words expresses the will to establish social relations, a consensus and agreement based on the word, and in our case, on the Basque language. As in Amazonia, in the Basque Country ceremonies like that would also constitute a space/moment in which to produce and reproduce that social question. The word, transformed into a social link, takes on a special force, in other words as a symbol of *mana*. One might speculate that Xalbador managed to turn whistles of derision into applause with the help of that special force (*mana*); one might speculate that the word manages to influence reality and transform reality itself by

---

us on waves hitting the shore (which can also be rough)." As Asier Altuna once said in an interview, this description is at the root of the documentary *Bertsolari* and, naturally, one can see it "performed" in the film itself.

means of that force, as Zulaika himself highlights (1988, 230): "Words 'do' things for people who 'do' them not only in speech but also in their lives."

One can find emotions at the root of that force and, alongside emotions—and as already stated—consensus and agreement.

What happens when criticism—in this case, from the gender perspective or stemming from feminism—emerges? What happens when non-shared emotions, wishes, and desires appear in this issue?

Basque culture has also trained the bertsolari physically in order to be the center of perception. If she or he has to be the voice of the people, the bertsolari must embrace, internalize, and, as a final objective, represent the popular will, so that the power of the word and the bertso may bring about change. Indeed, the bertsolari, the word (the Basque language) would internalize that power to do things in life via such activity. In order to do so she or he must be prepared by developing a special skillful sensibility. Technique alone is not enough, nor is well-developed discourse; if the bertsolari manages to get her or his voice heard, amid the whirlwind of outside noise, she or he will feel a sense of security and everything will be in order.[11] Yet, starting with the Xalbador incident, we realize that for women bertsolariak it is not just enough to note the popular will and to transform that into truth; they should also have the ability to take part in that will, when called for—as in Xalbador's case—in order to be able

---

11. These are the words of the bertsolari in the abovementioned interview, which I have edited.

to transform, change, or at least adapt it. But in order to do that they must speak from the heart, from the body, and still today in the Basque context, female bodies have not found a bertso home.

Bibliography

Aire, Fernando. 2006. *Odolaren mintzoa.* Zarautz: Auspoa.

Apalategi, Joxemartin. 1987. *Introducción a la historia oral.* Barcelona: Anthropos.

Azurmendi, Joxe. 1990. "Bertsolaritzaren kontzeptuari buruz." In Fito Rodríguez et al. *Bertsolaritza, formarik gabeko heziketa.* Bilbao: UPV-EHU.

Azurmendi, Mikel. 1993. *Nombrar, embrujar (para una historia del sometimiento de la cultura oral en el País Vasco).* Irun: Alberdania.

Berger, John. 1972. *Ways of Seeing.* London: Penguin.

Canepa, Gisela, ed. 2001. *Identidades representadas, experiencia y memoria en los Andes.* Lima: Fondo Editorial de la PUCP- Pontificia Universidad Católica del Perú.

Del Valle, Teresa, coord. 2002. *Modelos emergentes en los sistemas y las relaciones de género.* Madrid: Narcea.

Douglas, Mary. [1966] 1991. *Purity and Danger: An Analysis of Concepts of Pollution and Taboo.* New York: Praeger.

Esteban, Mari Luz. 2004. *Antropología del cuerpo. Género, itinerarios corporales, identidad y cambio.* Barcelona: Bellaterra.

———. 2009. "Cuerpos y políticas feministas." Paper presented at the Jornadas Estatales feministas de Granada (December 5–7, 2009). Available online at: http://www.caps.cat/images/stories/ Mari_Luz_Esteban_cuerpos.pdf (accessed June 6, 2016).

Fernández Poncela, Anna María. 2011. "Antropología de las emociones y teoría de los sentimientos." *Revista Versión Nueva Época* 26: 1–24.

Flores Martos, Juan Antonio. 2010. "Trabajo de campo etnográfico y gestión emocional: notas epistemológicas y metodológicas." *Ankulegi* 14: 11–23.

Foley, John. 1991. *Immanent Art: From Structure to Meaning in Traditional Oral Epic.* Bloomington and Indianapolis: Indiana University Press.

Garzia, Joxerra, Jon Sarasua, and Andoni Egaña. 2001. *The Art of Bertsolaritza: Improvised Basque Verse Singing.* Donostia: Bertsozale Elkartea.

Gaztelumendi, Beñat. 2010. "Nagore Soroa: Abiatu beharko genuke ikasle bakoitzak dauzkan ezaugarrietatik." *Bertsolari* 78: 18–33.

Huerta Rosas, Abigail. 2008. "La construcción social de los sentimientos desde Pierre Bourdieu." *Iberoforum: Revista de Ciencias Sociales de la Universidad Iberoamericana* 5, Year 3 (January–June 2008): 1–11.

Ingold, Tim. 2000. *The Perception of the Environment: Essays on Livelihood, Dwelling and Skill.* London and New York: Routledge.

Larrañaga, Carmen. 1994. "Bertsolarismo: habitat de la masculinidad." *Bitarte* 4: 29–51.

———. 1995 . "Andra bertsolarien historia." *Bertsolari* 17: 17–20.

————. 1997. "Del bertsolarismo silenciado." *Jentilbaratz* 6: 57–73.

Le Breton, David. 2006. *El sabor del mundo.* Buenos Aires: Nueva Visión.

———. 2013. "Por una antropología de las emociones." *Revista Latinoamericana de Estudios sobre Cuerpos, Emociones y Sociedad* 10, Year 4 (December 2012–March 2013): 69–79.

Lekuona, Manuel. 1978. *Ahozko literatura. Kardaberaz Bilduma.* Vitoria-Gasteiz: Librería Técnica de Difusión.

O' Brien O'Keeffe, Katherine.1998. "The Performing Body on the Oral-Literate Continuum: Old English Poetry." In John Miles Foley, ed. *Teaching Oral Traditions.* New York: The Modern Language Association.

Oteiza, Jorge. 2007. *Quousque Tandem.* Navarra: Fundación Museo Oteiza.

Quick, Catherine. 2011. "The Metonym: Rhetoric and Oral Tradition at the Crossroads." *Oral Tradition* 26, no. 2: 597–600.

Surrallés, Alexandre. 1998. "Entre el pensar y el sentir. La antropología frente a las emociones." *Anthropologica* 16: 291–304.

————. 2002–2003. "De la percepción en antropología. Algunas reflexiones sobre la noción de persona desde los estudios amazónicos." *Indiana* 19–20: 59–72.

————. 2003. "Face to Face: Meaning, Feeling and Perception in Amazonian Welcoming Ceremonies." *Journal of the Royal Anthropological Institute* 9, no. 4: 775–91.

————. 2009a. *En el corazón del sentido.* Lima: IFEA/IWGIA.

————. 2009b. "De la intensidad o los derechos del cuerpo. La afectividad como objeto y como método." *Runa* 1: 29–44.

White, Linda. 2001. "Orality and Basque Nationalism: Dancing with the Devil or Waltzing into the Future?" *Oral Tradition* 16, no. 1: 3–28.

Zulaika, Joseba. 1988. *Basque Violence: Metaphor and Sacrament.* Reno and Las Vegas: University of Nevada Press.

————. 2008. "Etnografías del deseo: bases teóricas." In *Retos teóricos y nuevas practices,* ed. Margaret Bullen and Carmen Díez. Donostia: Ankulegi.

4

Crossroad: Tradition and Modernity in the Improvised Song of the Catalan Countries

Josep Vicent Frechina

Let me, first of all, give a brief digression on the cultural context in which this work is circumscribed. The Catalan Countries is a name used for the administrative territories with a Catalan-speaking majority, which includes the regions of the Valencian Community, the Balearic Islands, Catalonia and the so-called Franja de Aragón (literally "Aragonese Strip"), all of these in Spain; the Principality of Andorra; and Northern Catalonia—an area that largely corresponds to the French department of the Pyrenees Orientales. The denomination was put forth in the 1960s by Valencian intellectual Joan Fuster, although it had been used occasionally in the late nineteenth and early twentieth centuries, and was quickly adopted by the progressive and linguistically conscious sectors of the population throughout all these territories. It is, however, a political concept that today is hotly debated for a variety of reasons—even in the most pro-independence regions of Catalonia—and that arouses visceral opposing reactions in the Valencian, Balearic, and Aragonese territories.

Nevertheless, although the consolidation of the autonomous state (the political system based on regional autonomy in the Spanish state) has had perverse consequences that have hindered the normality of cultural flows between Catalan-speaking territories, it has been in the field of culture and, especially, in popular music, where the evidence of a frame of reference that transcends administrative boundaries—and that clearly outlined the controversial cartographic shape—has been more pronounced. Specifically, many of the new dynamics that have developed around the improvised song in recent years have been framed territorially, culturally, and, more important, ideologically, in the context of the Catalan Countries—including even the protagonists of some of the improvised verses themselves (Schmitt Solà 2013). Hence the inescapable need to use the same field of reference in the analysis of such dynamics, beyond political controversy and spurious uses of the identity question.

Genres of Improvised Song in the Catalan Countries

If we started a journey from south to north in order to prepare an inventory of the different types of improvised song that have been used in the Catalan Countries,[1] we would find a very varied sample with

1. A more detailed description of all the genera listed below can be found in Vicent Frechina, 2014, 115-166) and in the literature quoted therein.

some genera virtually extinct—or fossilized in practices that have lost their improvised character—and others that preserve an outstanding vitality.

Beginning with the southern regions of Alicante, we first observe the recurrent presence of the last examples of *trovo* (Mas i Miralles 1983), a genre of improvised song very much implanted throughout the southeastern Iberian Peninsula—from the foothills of the Alpujarras region in Andalusia to the Cartagena countryside and the plain of Murcia.

The *comarcas*[2] of the Marina in the south and the Plana de Castelló in the north mark the limits of maximum diffusion of the Valencian genres improvised by antonomasia: the *cant d'estil* (literally, "singing of style") and the *albaes* ("dawn songs") (Frechina 2005; Marzal Barberà 2009;). Both genres are in full force in their traditional form. *Cant d'estil* and *albaes*, grouped occasionally under the generic name of *cant valencià*, are two independent musical genres that, however, go hand in hand because they are sung by the same singers in the same context—nocturnal rounds, called *guitarraes* in the first case and *nits d'albaes* in the second. An important peculiarity of both genres is that the singer himself rarely improvises the verses he sings, but they are dictated to the singer's ear by a specialist called the *versador*.

The *albaes* are sung by two singers who alternate their intervention. They are accompanied by the *dolçaina* and *tabal*—pipe and drum. The albaes are made up of four or five verses distributed in six

---

2. In Valencia and Catalonia, *comarca* is a local administrative division.

musical phrases, with three of each sung by one of the singers.

The *cant d'estil* is sung accompanied by a mixed ensemble formed by string and wind instruments—the guitar, *guitarró*, trumpet, clarinet, and trombone—although it is not unusual to pair the wind instruments with other stringed instruments, such as the *bandúrria* and the lute. The *cant d'estil* has diverse styles that are recognized by their different introduction and harmonic structure: *u i dos* and *u i dotze*, with the rhythmic structure of a fandango and alternation of tonic and dominant in the instrumental accompaniment; and *u* and *riberenca*—pertaining both to the fertile tree of the Andalusian fandangos. The numerical appellations given to these—"one and two," "one and twelve," and "one"—have never been satisfactorily explained, although most hypotheses are associated with dance steps or chord positions on the guitar.

A very important musical characteristic of the *cant d'estil* is the contrast between the instrumental accompaniment, which is of a tonal nature and regular rhythm, and the singing, which is of clear modal filiation and free rhythm. Such a contrast reinforces the vocal expressiveness of the interpretation, further propitiated by a certain improvisational freedom in the melody tracing, a strategic projection of the melismata—especially on the last syllable of each musical phrase—and a tendency to impregnate the phrasing with the pathos of the "mi mode," so present throughout the Mediterranean area.[3]

---

3. For the pathos associated with "mi mode," see Reig Bravo (2011, 245).

In the Catalan regions around the River Ebro we find another kind of improvised song that has a certain kinship with the Valencian *cant d'estil*: the currently termed *jotes del Ebre* (previously known as the *jota tortosina*), an appellation that reveals the displacement of identity the territory has experienced in recent years and that has been catalyzed, among other phenomena, by social protest against the National Hydrological Plan.[4] Like the cant d'estil, these improvised *jotes* are accompanied by a mixed ensemble of string and wind instruments, although in this case it is the *bombardino* that completes the triad of wind instruments together with trumpet and clarinet.[5]

The Ebro regions also mark the southern border of the expansion of the *cançons de pandero* (tambourine songs), a genre historically associated with the Majorelle of the Virgin of the Rosary who played them, accompanied by a square tambourine, in the festive desserts to raise funds for their *cofradia*. It is the only genre of improvised song in the Catalan Countries interpreted exclusively by women and spread throughout inland Catalonia to the northern slopes of the Pyrenees, already in Northern Catalonia. It fell into disuse during the first third of the twentieth century and has recently been recovered outside its traditional context (Serra i Boldú 1907 [1982]; Sistac i Sanvicén 1997; Palomar i Abadia 2004).

---

4. The Spanish National Hydrological Plan (NHP), approved in the year 2000, envisaged an important water transfer from the River Ebro to the Mediterranean coastal regions.
5. For a detailed description of this typology of *jotas* see Castellanos et al. (2010, 2011) and Ferré Pavia (2004).

The *corrandes de caramelles*, included in the Easter ritual, were also widely disseminated through much of Catalonia (Roviró 2010). They are sung by a specialized *corrandista* during the round that is carried out by the houses and farms of the population on Easter Saturday.

Two other genres, the *nyacres* and *patacades*, are limited exclusively to a few Empordian populations: with the *nyacres* in Roses, Castelló d'Empúries, and Sant Pere Pescador; and the *patacades* in Cadaqués. In both cases they are songs that accompany collective dances. The *nyacres* disappeared many years ago, but they have been revived successfully within the new contexts in which the improvised song is practiced today. On the contrary, the *patacades* are still interpreted within the ritual sequence of the San Sebastián feast day in Cadaqués.

Another type of implementation that is strictly local in origin is the *garrotín*, which is limited to the Romani communities in the city of Lleida (Tort and López 2003). They were sung—and danced—in festive gatherings, private parties, and Carnival celebrations. They have, therefore, a funny and naughty tone—*carrincló,* in the slang of the city.

All genres mentioned so far have a similar poetic structure: octosyllabic verses grouped in stanzas ranging from four verses for the simplest combinations and six for the more sophisticated ones—although tambourine songs usually duplicate the four-line stanza. The rhymes go equally from the required minimum of rhyming assonant of the even verses to the complete rhyme consonant of the alternate verses.

We find greater freedom of versifying in the *glosa* of the Balearic Islands (Sbert i Garau 2009). In Mallorca, the *glosa* is sung without instrumental accompaniment. Historically, each singer had his/her own characteristic melody. The Mallorcan *glosa* has a significant strophic flexibility, so that the *glosador* can adapt the number of verses to his/her expressive needs, from a minimum of four to a maximum that rarely exceeds twelve. It is usually interpreted as a poetic combat that defends opposite positions, represents antagonistic roles, or is simply dialogue singing.

In Menorca, the *glosa* is accompanied by a guitar melody called *ses porgueres*. Its basic stanza is six verses in ABBAAB rhyme, but it is not difficult to find other combinations of seven to twelve verses with different rhyming patterns. It is also interpreted in the form of a combat between several *glosadors* (López Casasnova 2007; Pons 2003; Tur 2013).

In Majorca there is another widespread genre of improvised song that is sung, usually, around the bonfires in the festival of San Antonio: the songs of *ximbomba*(the friction drum), in which it is easy to see the alternation between so-called contextual improvisation—memorized stanzas that are integrated into an improvised dialogue—and pure improvisation (Ayats 2010).

Crossroad

In the early 1980s, the deep socioeconomic transformations of the last third of the twentieth century led to the definitive collapse of a more traditional

society—with the consequent growth of urban live-
lihoods to the detriment of those in the rural world
and the progressive abandonment of the agricultural
calendar and its associated rituals.

At this point, out of all the different types of improvised song in the Catalan Countries, the only ones
that maintained a certain validity were the *glosa* of
Mallorca and Menorca, the *jotes* of the Ebro, and the
Valencian *albaes* and *cant d'estil*. There were very few
singers of *corrandes*, with Josep Casadevall *Carolino*
being the best known of these (Roviró 2005); some
genres had practically ceased to be performed, like
the *garrotín*, for example; and others had disappeared completely, as in the case of the tambourine
songs or *nyacres*.

At the time in València there were still a few
active *versadors* like Paco Ortí (1940–2013), Enric
Gironés (1950), Manuel Marzal, known as *el Xiquet
de Mislata* (1918–1993), Josep Bahilo (1940–2011),
Vicent Izquierdo *Naiet de Bétera* (1949), and Josep
Estellés *el Xiquet del Carme* (1937–2016); all of them,
except the first two, were also singers who kept alive
a cultural expression that was losing some of its rel-
evance in the festive framework and was beginning
to be relegated to a "folkloric citadel," increasingly
hemmed into a much reduced social and cultural
space.

In the territories of the Ebro, the charisma of Josep
García *Canalero* (1914–2004) shone brightly, accom-
panied by Francisco Roig *lo Noro* (1905–2002), José
Guarch *Teixidor* (1931–2011), and Andreu Queralt
Codonyol (1925–1989) (Rovira 2002).

In Menorca the *glosa* was in a bad way with the withdrawal or disappearance of the old generation of *glosadors* headed by Antoni Olives *l'amo de Son Mascaró* (1909–1981), Josep Triay (1907–1983), and Llorenç Janer *Vivetes* (1902–1993). Fortunately, the capital figure of Miquel Ametller (1937) began to emerge (Pons 2005). Alongside Esteve Barceló *Verderol* (1946), her would be decisive in the future of the *glosa*.

Finally, as in the rest of the cases referred to above, there was no generational rejuvenation within the *glosa* of Mallorca and the old active *glosadors* found themselves to be the last link in a traditional chain that was about to break. They were, among others, Joana Serra *Cartera* (1908–1991), Miquel Perelló *Canta* (1915–1990), Joan *Planisi* (1928), Antoni Socias *Pobler* (1929–2011), and Rafel Roig *Carritxoner* (1933–2017).

The slow languishing of traditional genres propitiated by the dynamics of developmentalism and mass culture would be interrupted, however, by a countercurrent that would recover some practices typical of traditional society, but recontextualize them with new functionalities within the framework of an advanced modern society.

This was the case of the improvised song that initiated a process of revitalization in territories in which it seemed condemned to disappear, that redoubled its validity where it had not yet entered decay, and that was reborn seemingly from nowhere and encouraged by the unveiling of traditional music, as a kind of identity marker, which occurred in urban areas under the umbrella of new folk music.

These three phenomena—revival, intensification, and recreation—occurred in varying degrees throughout the territories, but they were developed following more or less common patterns: the movements started simultaneously, were animated by the dynamic action of cultural associationism, and inevitably interbred, giving rise to interesting synergies and occasional conflicts.

In Menorca, for example, a decisive event in 1999 was the founding of Soca de Mots, an association that would bring together all the active *glosadors* on the island and that would capitalize on initiatives to promote and teach the *glosat*.

In Mallorca, the body that initially assumed this same role was the Canonge de Santa Cirga cultural association in Manacor, which, with the encouragement of Felip Munar and Mateu Llodrá, organized the Regional Glosat Shows and gave way to the foundation, in 2008, of the Associació de Glosadors de Mallorca. Felip Munar is also the author of two important didactic books that are widely used in *glosa* workshops that have spread throughout the Balearic territory (Munar 2001, 2008).

The point of inflection was marked in Valencia by two significant events: the publication of Carles Pitarch's initial research (Pitarch 1997), which for the first time introduced the notion of the cultural and artistic value of the *cant d'estil* and the *albaes* from an academic approach; and, above all, the publication, by the Fonoteca de Materials of the

Generalitat Valenciana (the Valencian government), of the *Antologia del Cant Valencià d'Estil (1915–1996)* (1997). The creation of the Godella singing schools of Godella, in which the singer Josep Aparicio Apa exercises his mastery, and the Popular University of València, with Victoria Sousa *Victorieta* as a main reference, would also play a significant role.

In Catalunya, where the improvised song only retained an important presence in the regions of the River Ebro, the phenomenon of recreation would be especially transcendent. A careful analysis of its timeline demonstrates three obvious milestones.

First, there was the creation of the Tradicionàrius festival in Barcelona in 1988. Tradicionàrius has been the main supporter of the folk movement in the Catalan Countries and its powerful influence has been felt throughout the territory. For example, one of the groups popularized by the festival, Quico el Célio, Noi and Mut de Ferreries, has popularized the improvised *jotas,* and some of their most emblematic interpreters such as Canalero or Teixidor, outside of their natural environment. Moreover, encounters of singers promoted by festivals that mirrored the Tradicionàrius—like that organized by the Solc association in the region of Lluçanès, for example—would promote some *corrandistas* like Carolino de Folgueroles; the same Tradicionàrius would also support improvised song get-togethers that, under the denomination of Corrandàrius, encouraged the career of Francesc Tomàs Panxito; and many bands and performers at the same festival, like Marcel Casellas, De Calaix, Pomada, and their specialized incarnation, Ensaladilla So Insistent, would incorporate improvised song into their repertoires.

The second milestone was the publication in 2002 of the specialized fanzine *Cor de Carxofa*—behind which are some members of bands mentioned above—and the subsequent foundation of the association of the same name in 2006 that, in a short time, has become the most important reference point for the improvised song in Catalunya: Cor de Carxofa organizes workshops for initiation into the world of improvisation as well as program meetings and festivals, and it enjoys an important position in the network, publishing a *Manual d'Iniciació a la Glosa* (2008) which laid the foundations for a new way of understanding improvised song based on the *transglosador* model: in other words, an improviser without genre or geographical markers that uses the different genres as interchangeable expressive resources and that, therefore, can also improvise on *glosa* from Menorca, on *nyacra* from l'Empurdà, on jota from the Ebro territories, or on Valencian *albaes*.

This model was definitively consolidated with the third of the three milestones mentioned above: the creation of the Trobada de Cantadors ("Singers Meeting") of Espolla (2004), inspired by the Basque competitions of *bertsolaris*, in which the winner is proclaimed with the crown of Nyacres King/Queen (Tegido-Mallart *Gustinet* 2012). This meeting facilitated the media visibility of a new improvised song that would henceforth be called, generically, *glosa*: a controversial metonymic operation that, however, has been quite successful and very quickly implemented.

Under the impulse of Cor de Carxofa, and taking advantage of the popular success of the Trobada de Cantadors, different events were organized such as the improvisers' championship leagues and twelve hours of improvised song. The model thus spread rapidly throughout the territory: popular institutions, cultural associations, and civic entities of all kinds and conditions organized the singing of *nyacres*, battles of *garrotins*, *glosa* afternoons, nights of *corrandes*, and so on. At these events, new improvisers came to coexist occasionally with singers from a more traditional background, with a notable presence of young Mallorcan and Menorcan poets who combined both traditional and modern formats. Mateu Matas *Xurí* (Frechina 2013) and Maribel Servera *Servereta* would be the most paradigmatic examples: both have won the Espolla contest without ceasing to be two of the primary exponents of the present Majorcan traditional *glosa*. Their poetry, however, has undergone notable changes with respect to the traditional poetry bequeathed to them by previous generations: their melodic palette has expanded considerably and it is not difficult to perceive in them the influence of the vigorous Ibero-American movement around the improvised *décima* (ten-line stanza) in its preference for this structure or in the adoption of a final *seguidilla* with which, in the way of the great Alexis Diaz *Pimienta*, Xurí brightly closes his interventions.

The above example is not the only consequence of the confluence of modern and traditional practices. There have also been, as mentioned earlier, small conflicts owing to the overlapping of the multigeneric and participatory dynamics that are promoted in the new contexts with their more traditional counterparts, which have always operated under different formulas.

In the new dynamics priority is given to the playful aspect, to the open and collective celebration that is developed over new rituals, with the musical component dissociated from the text and converted into an accessory and interchangeable element. If this is done with genres that have fallen into disuse, such as tambourine songs or *nyacres*, the operation is innocuous and has no collateral effects. However, if it is done with living genres that are consequently decontextualized and, in a sense, perceived as distorted, it is possible to generate a certain amount of discomfort among habitual listeners: it is not difficult to understand the perplexity with which a veteran *glosador* from Menorca or a Valencian singer contemplates those willing *gloses* or *albaes* that appear, more or less disfigured—to say nothing of the instrumental accompaniment, or the tuning, or the pitch, or the placement of the voice, or the circumstances, or the customary ritual surrounding the *jotes*, *corrandes*, and *garrotins*. I assume, however, that it is time to accept this collectivization of a heritage that was understood up to now as exclusive to specific owners who are its new custodians.

Another problematic consequence of the overlapping of dynamics, and one that is a little more complex than the previous point, is observed by Anaís Falcó (2014) in regard to the feast day of Sant Sebastián of Cadaqués in which occasional improvised *patacades*

are sung. In recent years, the success of the improvised song has promoted among its new practitioners and adepts a certain cultural tourism whose
main impulse is to attend traditional rituals in which
improvisation plays a central role. This is not exactly
the case with the festival of Cadaqués because the *patacades* are rarely improvised, but are instead mostly
repeated in a ritual that "simulates" improvisation.
However, visitors try to intervene during the party
by improvising some stanzas or even interacting
with the "official" singer—Dionis Baró. This attitude
in turn disturbs the "genuine" participants and ends
up distorting the festive model of interest.

In any case, and despite these small clashes between two realities that are learning to coexist, the
new improvised song continues on its unstoppable
progression: it forms part of the pro-independence
imaginary in which it has become strongly rooted ,
especially among younger people that perceive it to
be a powerful instrument for articulating a collective identity as well as a vehicle of fun and valuable
communication; furthermore, it has entered with
force into the world of the education—for example,
the Corrandascola project designed by Albert Casals
is a magnificent example of the enormous potential
that this practice could have at school (Casals 2010;
Casals, Ayats, and Vilar 2010); and it has conquered
social networks in an imaginative and surprising way:
on January 22, 2011 the Twitter social network was
flooded with tweets with the hashtag #garrotweet as
a result of the invitation made by Oriol Beltran *Uru*,
who had written:

Perquè els folkis 2.0
no quedin en entredit
provoco el noi del Pandero
i inauguro el #garrotweet.

For the folkies 2.0
Do not be questioned
I provoke the tambourine boy
and I open the #garrotweet.

The move was made, in fact, to play with the double restriction of the maximum of 140 characters per tweet imposed by Twitter and the four octosyllabic verses of the traditional couplet—here linked to traditional genre of *garrotín*. Most significant, however, was not the abundant tweets, which remain, but the euphoria exhibited by participants in and editors of the numerous media that responded to it—a euphoria born from the feeling of conciliation and aroused by a game as harmless and banal as that described, between a well-established tradition and one of the most rabidly contemporary forms of communication.

Future Perspectives

Against this background, improvised song faces the twenty-first century in the Catalan Countries with a double reality at stake.

On the one hand, traditional practices resist the onslaught of modernization and regain lost social prestige even if their real presence in the cultural calendar has diminished. In the Valencian Country the *nits d'albaes* and the *guitarraes* of *cant d'estil* remain in their most important fiefdoms—El Puig, Bétera,

Xàtiva, the festival of the Fallas, and so on—but their frequency has waned in the rest of their territory. The Associació d'Estudis del Cant Valencià (2008) has been founded, and there are several active *versadors* such as Paco Nicasio *Paco de Faura*, Josemi Sánchez, Salvador López *Voro de Paterna*, Vicent Ribelles *Vicent de Rosa*, and Carles Bahilo; the schools of *cant d'estil* have experienced an important growth and, in a decision debated by certain authors that do not believe it to be the most suitable option (Reig Bravo 2014), the Council of Ministers approved, in June 2014, a royal decree that created the specialty of *cant valencià* in professional schools of music. There is, however, no school of verses that reinforces de facto the historical subordination of poetic improvisation to singing.

In the regions of the River Ebro there is a generation of young singers—José Subirats *Joseret*, Marc Guarch *Guardet*, Sofía Morales *Sofía de la Ribera*, and Sílvia Lluís *Sílvia Ampolla*—who improvise *jotas* in the traditional context: rounds, family celebrations, feasts, and so on. Initiatives such as the Escola de Música Tradicional Ebrenca lo Canalero (2015) have been launched in Roquetes, which organized the first course of improvised song in Catalan—with healthy representation from all the improvised genres of the Catalan Countries. Additionally, the Centre d'Interpretació de la Jota de les Terres de l'Ebre - Casa de la Jota (2013) has been opened in Tortosa. And, since 2013, the Ebrefolk, Campus de Música i Balls Populars de les Terres de l'Ebre, and the Jotacampus, the summer school of the Aula de

Músiques de la Terra have been taking place, disseminating and teaching the improvised jota.

In Mallorca and Menorca the situation is even more positive. There are dozens of *glosadors* and *glosa* enjoys a constant presence in the media. In 2015, according to data from the website of the Association of *Glosadors* of Mallorca, there were *glosa* shows on almost one hundred days of the year, a significant part of them in bars and restaurants, which indicates its ability to attract the public (Vicens 2012). A recent census of *glosadors de picat* in Majorca (Munar 2015)—poets capable of executing a poet fight or battle—records twenty-four names, among which include the aforementioned Mateu Xurí and Maribel Servera, together with Macià Ferrer *Noto*, Antònia Nicolau *Pipiu*, Toni Llull *Carnisser*, Antoni Viver *Mostel*, Jordi Cloquell *Artiller*, Miquel Àngel Adrover *Campaner*, and Llorenç Màgic *Cloquell*. And from Menorca we can also mention Bep Coll, Moisès Coll *Zès*, Alfonso de la Llana, Joan Fortuny *Nanis*, Bep Guàrdia, Joan Moll *Joanet*, Pons Pons, Toni Rotger, Paco Rotger, and Miquel Truyol.

On the other hand, the new improvised song maintains its firm pulse: Cor de Carxofa inaugurated, with great enrollment success, the Escola d'Estiu de Glosa in Espolla (2012) as a prelude to the Trobada de Cantadors; and the same association has been able to establish some fixed appointments in the calendar—for example, *glosa* Wednesdays in the Ateneu de Manlleu and the itinerant *glosa* workshops, also on Wednesdays, in the Gracia neighborhood of Barcelona. And only recently a new amateur *glosa* championship has been launched—the ABBA league, organized by the FIGA (Federació Intercomarcal de Glosa Amateur)—which is expected to run from three to five days.

Consequently, if the traditional dynamics assure the territorial roots and the existence of genuine referents in improvised song, modern dynamics can play a cohesive and dynamic role that connects the improvisation of the different territories, provides new values, and brings them to areas that the former could hardly achieve alone. The mutual reinforcement between both dynamics allows us to foresee, then, at least in the short term, a future as open as it is promising.

Bibliography

Ayats, Jaume. 2010. "Cantar allò que no es pot dir. Les cançons de sant Antoni a Artà, Mallorca." *Trans: Revista Transcultural de Música* 14. At http://www.sibetrans.com/trans/article/19/cantar-allo-que-no-es-pot-dir-les-cancons-de-sant-antoni-a-arta-mallorca (accessed February 7, 2017).

Casals, Albert, ed. 2010. *Corrandescola: Proposta didàctica per treballar la glosa a Primària.* Cerdanyola del Vallès: ICE-UAB.

Casals, Albert, Jaume Ayats, and Mercé Vilar. 2010. "Improvised Song in Schools: Breaking Away from the Perception of Traditional Song as Infantile by Introducing a Traditional Adult Practice." *Oral Tradition* 25, no 2: 365–80. At http://journal.oraltradition.org/issues/25ii/casals (accessed February 7, 2017).

Castellanos, Eva, Cinta Martí, M. Carme Queralt, Roc Salvadó, and Joan Francesc Vidal. 2010. "La jota improvisada cantada a les terres de l'Ebre." *Revista d'Etnologia de Catalunya* 35: 217–20.

———. 2011. "La jota improvisada a les terres de l'Ebre." *Caramella* 24 (January–June): 4–7.

Cor de Carxofa. 2008. *Manual d'iniciació a la glosa.* Barcelona: Associació Cor de Carxofa.

Falcó, Anaís. 2014. "El basilisc de música i festa: El cas de Sant Sebastià a Cadaqués." *Caramella* 30 (January–June): 86–88.

Ferré Pavia, Carme. 2004. *"Cantadors de l'Ebre. La jota improvisada en el Baix Ebre i el Montsià."* In *Encuentro sobre la improvisación oral en el mundo (Donostia, 2003-11-3/8).* Donostia: Euskal Herriko Bertsozale Elkartea.

Frechina, Josep Vicent. 2005. "El 'cant d'estil' valenciano." *Etno-folk. Revista galega d'etnomuxicologia* 3 (November): 85–88.

———. 2011. *La cançó en valencià. Dels repertoris tradicionals als gèneres moderns.* València: Acadèmia Valenciana de la Llengua.

———. 2013. "Mateu Xurí. Mestre de la paraula." *Caramella* 28 (January–June): 66–69.

———. 2014. *Pensar en vers. La cançó improvisada als Països de la Mediterrània.* Calaceit: Llibres de Caramella.

López Casasnova, Joan F. 2007. "Poesia popular: els glosadors a Menorca." *Anuari Verdaguer* 15: 373–407.

Marzal Barberà, Manuel. 2009. "El Xiquet de Mislata." In *Materials inèdits per a una antologia del cant valencià*, edited by Carles A. Pitarch Alfonso. València: Museu Valencià d'Etnologia.

Mas i Miralles, Antoni. 1983. "Aproximació a l'estudi del trobo a Santa Pola." *La Rella* 1: 13–32.

Munar, Felip. 2001. *Manual del bon glosador: Tècniques, exercicis i glosades.* Palma de Mallorca: Documenta Balear.

———. 2008. *Jo vull ésser glossador.* Palma: Documenta Balear.

———. 2015. *Els glosadors de picat a Mallorca.* Palma: Documenta Balear.

Palomar i Abadia, Salvador. 2004. "Les cançons de pandero. Música i ritual." *Caramella* 10 (January–June): 21–26.

Pitarch Alfonso, Carles A. 1997. "El cant valencià d'estil: Apunts per a un estudi conceptual i històric." In *El món del cant*, addenda to *l'Antologia del cant valencià d'estil (1915–1996)*. València: Generalitat Valenciana, Conselleria de Cultural, Educació i Ciència; Editorial la Máscara.

Pons, Llúcia. 2003. "Va de glosat." *Caramella* 8 (January–June): 48–52.

———. 2005. "Miquel Ametller, «mestre» de glosadors." *Caramella* 12 (January–June): 10–15.

Reig Bravo, Jordi. 2011. *La música tradicional valenciana. Una aproximació etnomusicològica*, València: Institut Valencià de la Música.

———. 2014. "L'ensenyament del cant d'estil als conservatoris professionals." *Notas de paso* 1: 121–29. At http://revistadigital2.csmvalencia.es/wp-content/uploads/2016/02/Revista-1-PDF.pdf.

Rovira, Joan-Josep. 2002. *Cantadors del Delta. Teixidor, Lo Noro, Caragol.* Tortosa: Cinctorres Club.

Roviró, Xavier. 2005. "El corrandista Josep Casadevall i Sangles, *Carolino.*" *Caramella* 12 (January–June): 16–20.

———. 2010. "Les corrandes de camalleres. Cançons improvisades d'humor, sàtira i crítica." *Caramella* 23 (January–June): 124–27.

Sbert i Garau, Miquel. 2000. "La poesia improvisada en las Illes Balears: los 'glosadors.'" In *Actas del VI Encuentro-Festival Iberoamericano de la Décima y el Verso Improvisado*, edited by Maximiano Trapero et al. Las Palmas de Gran Canaria: Universidad de Las Palmas de Gran Canaria.

———. 2009. *Llengua de glosador. Notes sobre poesía de tradició oral.* Palma: Lleonard Muntaner.

Schmitt Solà, Bàrbara. 2013. "*O cantem o desapareixem.* La glosa i els Països Catalans." *Mirmanda* 8: 74–80.

Serra i Boldú, Valeri. 1907 [1982]: *Cançons de pandero. Cançons de ronda.* Arxiu de Tradicions Populars. Facsimile edition. Barcelona and Palma de Mallorca: José J. de Olañeta.

Sistac i Sanvicén, Dolors. 1997. *Les cançons de pandero o de tambor. Estudi i noves aportacions.* Lleida: Institut d'Estudis Ilerdencs.

Tegido-Mallart *Gustinet*, Josep Maria. 2012. "Pomada de cor de carxofa dins de(l) calaix." *Caramella* 27 (July–December): 115–16.

Tort, Josep, and Matías López. 2003. *Lo garrotín de Lleida: Sintonia d'una ciutat de paios i gitanos.* Lleida: Ajuntament de Lleida.

Tur, Aina. 2013. *La glosa menorquina (anàlisi contemporània del glosat i els glosadors.* Quaderns de Folklore 98. Ciutadella: Collectiu Folklòric de Ciutadella.

Vicens, Francesc. 2011. "Reinventar la tradició. Nous usos del glosat a Mallorca." *Caramella* 25: 15–18.

Singer Karen Owen. Photo by Conny Beyreuther.
Courtesy of Xenpelar Dokumentazio Zentroa.

Researcher Josep Vincent Frechina. Photo by Xenpelar
Dokumentazio Zentroa.

Singers Yunet López and Alaia Martin. Photo by Conny Beyreuther. Courtesy of Xenpelar Dokumentazio Zentroa.

Singers Mateu Xuri and Maribel Servera. Photo by Conny Beyreuther. Courtesy of Xenpelar Dokumentazio Zentroa.

Alaia Martin and Maribel Servera. Photo by Conny Beyreuther. Courtesy of Xenpelar Dokumentazio Zentroa.

Maribel Servera and Maialen Lujanbio. Photo by Conny Beyreuther. Courtesy of Xenpelar Dokumentazio Zentroa.

*Participants of the conference on improvised singing in
Donostia-San Sebastián, Basque Country.
Photo by Conny Beyreuther. Courtesy of Xenpelar
Dokumentazio Zentroa.*

*Participants of the conference on improvised singing.
Photo by Xenpelar Dokumentazio Zentroa.*

Participants of the conference on improvised singing.
Photo by Xenpelar Dokumentazio Zentroa.

Researcher Albert Casals. Photo by Xenpelar
Dokumentazio Zentroa.

Performance of improvising poets in the aquarium.
Photo by Conny Beyreuther. Courtesy of Xenpelar
Dokumentazio Zentroa.

Bertsolari Beñat Gaztelumendi Arandia. Photo by
Alberto Elosegi. Courtesy of Xenpelar Dokumentazio
Zentroa .

Poet and researcher Eurig Salisbury. Photo by Xenpelar Dokumentazio Zentroa.

Researcher Harkaitz Zubiri. Photo by Xenpelar Dokumentazio Zentroa.

Researcher Jone Miren Hernandez. Photo by Xenpelar
Dokumentazio Zentroa.

Performance of Basque and Cypriot improvisers in
the streets of Oñati, Basque Country. Photo by Conny
Beyreuther. Courtesy of Xenpelar Dokumentazio Zentroa.

Performance of Welsh improviser Eurig Salisbury in the streets of Donostia-San Sebastián, Basque Country. Photo by Conny Beyreuther. Courtesy of Xenpelar Dokumentazio Zentroa.

Participants and organizers after the great festival of improvised poetry in the Kursaal of Donostia-San Sebastián, Basque Country. Photo by Conny Beyreuther. Courtesy of Xenpelar Dokumentazio Zentroa .

Austrian improvisers in full performance at the Kursaal.
Photo by Conny Beyreuther. Courtesy of Xenpelar
Dokumentazio Zentroa.

Cuban improvisers performing at the Kursaal.
Photo by Conny Beyreuther. Courtesy of Xenpelar
Dokumentazio Zentroa .

*Researcher Miren Artetxe. Photo by Xenpelar
Dokumentazio Zentroa.*

*Researcher Patricia Tapanes. Photo by Xenpelar
Dokumentazio Zentroa.*

Researcher Ruth Finnegan. Photo by Conny Beyreuther. Courtesy of Xenpelar Dokumentazio Zentroa.

Improvising performance at three corners in Tabakalera, Donostia-San Sebastián, Basque Country. Photo by Conny Beyreuther. Courtesy of Xenpelar Dokumentazio Zentroa.

Alondras Huastecas: Dana Sofía Limón, Rebeca Limón and Diana Laura Hernández. Photo by Conny Beyreuther. Courtesy of Xenpelar Dokumentazio Zentroa.

The participants dined daily in the Kresala Society, Donostia-San Sebastián, Basque Country. Photo by Xenpelar Dokumentazio Zentroa.

*Researcher Thierry Rougier. Photo by Xenpelar
Dokumentazio Zentroa.*

5

Singing Improvised Verses to Promote the Language in Schools: The Case of Catalonia

Albert Casals

Si voleu ballar corrandes
jo us en cantaré deu mil,
que les duc a la butxaca,
lligadetes amb un fil.

If you want to sing corrandes
there's ten thousand I can sing.
They're here in my pocket
well tied up with a thin string.

(traditional *corranda*)

In the last twenty years, the activities revolving around *corrandes*—songs with improvised verses—have gone from being a disappearing phenomenon to one of the most important assets of language and music with traditional roots in Catalonia today. This unexpected and accelerated growth has been accompanied by an increasing interest on the part of the Catalan education sector. But how has this phenomenon occurred?

In this chapter I will explain the introduction of corrandes in schools in Catalonia, focusing specifically on their impact on the use and survival of Catalan. To this end, I will first outline what corrandes are, the situation of the Catalan language, the school system in Catalonia, and the evolution of corrandes, as a necessary context for understanding the growth of this activity in the educational context described below. Second, I will briefly report on the work done in classrooms and then conclude by discussing the consequences and importance of such work for the adoption of Catalan as the habitual language of communication in Catalonia.

Some Notes on Catalan and the School System in Catalonia

Catalan is one of the Romance languages spoken in southwestern Europe, in the region known as the *Països Catalans*.[1] It is estimated that there are around ten million speakers, of whom 60 percent live in Catalonia (Plataforma per la Llengua 2016). It should be noted that Catalan is a stateless language and that Catalonia is one of the autonomous communities that make up Spain, although it is currently immersed in a political process of self-determination based on its language, culture, and character.[2]

While not wishing to go deeper into the situation of Catalan as the language commonly used in

---

1. To learn more about the history of Catalan, I recommend reading Vallverdú (1984) and Ionita (2017).
2. To understand the political situation in Catalonia, it is worth reading Lanz (2016).

Catalonia, nor having this possibility due to the constraints of space here, it does seem necessary to highlight some data that can help to illustrate the existing strengths, problems, and weaknesses of this supposition.

Drawing at all times on the latest report on the situation of Catalan, published by the Observatori de la Llengua (Xarxa CRUSCAT 2015), we find that:

Although the percentages of inhabitants who can understand, speak, read, and write in Catalan in Catalonia may be considered by many people as good or acceptable (95 percent, 73 percent, 79 percent, and 56 percent respectively), the data also show that in the ten years between 2003 and 2013, those who defined themselves as Catalan or bilingual by birth gradually decreased (by around 4 percent), while the number of Spanish speakers or those with another mother tongue increased (by 9.2 percent and 152.8 percent, respectively).

The data indicate the appeal held by Catalan: for example, there are more people who speak to their children in Catalan than to their mothers, and there are more people who state that Catalan is their language of habitual use than those who indicate that it is their mother tongue. In contrast, only 38.5 percent of the population said Catalan was their main language (L1) in 2014.

Both in the written press and radio, the offer in Catalan has grown steadily compared to Spanish. For its part, television in Catalan has maintained about 20 percent of the audience share over the last few years, although it should be underscored that the

Catalan public television channel, TV3, topped the audience ratings in 2015. On the other hand, only 3 to 4 percent of moviegoers choose to watch films in Catalan (although it is also true that the offer of films dubbed or subtitled in Catalan is low).

Given this scenario and the linguistic problems that exist in Catalonia—in which there is a struggle between a stateless language without effective recognition outside its territory and another official language with millions of speakers, favored by the state and receiving international recognition—compulsory schooling emerges as one of the decisive fields in which the weaker language plays out its future, and its very survival. Hence, in 1983 linguistic immersion in Catalan was introduced into the schools in Catalonia, an option that was later formalized by the 2009 Catalan Education Act[3]: "Catalan is the language normally used as the language of transmission and learning in the Education System" (Article 11.1).[4]

The model established by the aforesaid law is justified because it guarantees full mastery of the Catalan and Spanish languages on completing compulsory schooling (Article 10.1) and the non-segregation of

---

3. As the reader may well know, any discussion of the Spanish education system means referring not only to a series of general and common parameters throughout the territory that makes up Spain but also to a diversity of models that exist in the various regions that hold delegated competences in the field of education. One of these regions is the autonomous community of Catalonia.

4. The original legal text is: "El català és la llengua normalment emprada com a llengua vehicular i d'aprenentatge del sistema educatiu" (Llei 12/2009, d'Educació).

pupils in centers, classes, or groups for reasons of language (Article 11.3). This model, although it is supported by the results and praised as an example to follow outside Catalonia, is currently the object of attack by Spanish centralist sectors within the spiral of political controversy experienced in recent years.

The Corrandes and their Process of Positive Reevaluation and Revitalization

Having outlined the situation of Catalan and linguistic immersion in compulsory schooling, we must now consider the nature of corrandes and how they have evolved in Catalonia over the last fegw decades.

In the Catalan-speaking regions, the *Països Catalans*, Jaume Ayats (2007, 114–18) lists up to nineteen genres or classifications of songs with lyrics that are improvised over a sole melodic formula. Most of them have been present at some point in Catalonia, with the corranda being the most generalized form.[5] Historically, the term has often been used generically in Catalonia to define this type of repertoire, although it currently coexists alongside others: the descriptive "improvised song" or, more recently, *glosa*. This latter term is, in fact, a word from the Balearic Islands adopted to denominate any activity that develops around improvised poetry in Catalan, whatever its origins, the melody used, or the type of activity in course. In this chapter I use

---

5. Other forms worthy of note are the *jotes de l'Ebre*, the *garrotins*, and the *cançons de pandero*. To learn more about them and their background, I recommend reading Ayats (2007) and Frechina (2014).

the term corranda (or corrandes in the plural) as a way of making clear that I am only discussing what happens in the context of Catalonia.

Corrandes coincide with most similar genres in other cultures in the sense of being more than one type of song. I define their performance as an important communicative activity within the group in which it occurs (Ayats 2007, 66), with implications for the level of group identity (in the sense of Gross 2008) and often associated with ethnic affiliations (as described by White 2001). This is an oral, multimodal, communicative activity using spoken, musical, and body languages. And it is eminently social. As is usual in oral culture, improvised verses have value and meaning in the here and now, seeking to impact a live audience, without any pretension of creating poetry that will last over time. In particular, corrandes are based on melodies borrowed from their own cultural tradition or that have been popularized, and they usually have a playful character and/or feature social criticism (Ayats 2007).

If we go back to the 1980s and 1990s, we find scholars of folklore and traditional music warning of the imminent disappearance of the traditional songbook and its manifestations in Catalonia (Pujol 1985), among them the corrandes. In fact, there were still a few singers scattered around the region and possibly two areas where the art of improvisation through singing continued to show some signs of life: southern Catalonia (Terres de l'Ebre) with its *jotas*, and the Romani community in Lleida with the *garrotín*.

Nonetheless, it is common knowledge that tradition adapts to new circumstances and has a strong survival instinct. Accordingly, the activity of improvising sung verses was revalued positively and revitalized (see Frechina 2014 and Serrà 2005, 9–11). Like the traditions in many other places, the corranda was reinvented, mutating from something outmoded, for old and illiterate people living in rural contexts, to something modern, typical of young urbanites with university studies (Casals, Ayats, and Vilar 2010).

In this new stage, which began at the turn of the century, it is important to note that the impetus behind the new *corrandes* came from the world of music. It emerged in certain folk music scenes and was later channeled through the *Cor de Carxofa* association. Although this situation has subsequently evolved, in this context the preponderance of musicians as compared to philologists, lyricists, or other wordsmiths is still evident. This is something particular to Catalonia and it reoccurred with the introduction of corrandes into schools.

Their growth in the last decade has been astounding;indeed, it could almost be described as exponential: the number of events and singers has soared; the *Cor de Carxofa* association has grown significantly both in terms of activities and supporters; their social impact and media coverage has increased considerably; and there are people who work or who intend to work—even if only part-time—in the field of corrandes. Specifically, one of the areas in which more progress has been made and is anticipated is education: from the training of *corrandistes* (cor-randes singers) in workshops and on courses to the implementation of school and interschool corranda projects.[6]

Corrandes and Schools: A Successful Partnership

The presence of corrandes in schools in Catalonia is a relatively recent phenomenon, but in just a few years they have found a place on the Catalan education agenda. Following a few isolated and non-systematized trials, a first pilot project was carried out in a primary school in the 2006–2007 school year, which was repeated the following year with four more. The excellent results obtained and compiled in the form of a dissertation (Casals 2009) led in 2009–2010 to the development of the *Corrandescola* (corrandes for schools) program. Subsequent to the publication of the didactic pro-posal (Casals 2010), specific training courses were set up with the support of the Servei d'Immersió i Ús de la Llengua.[7] These have currently been pi-loted directly in more than forty schools. Indirectly, through teacher training, we also know that many more schools are experimenting with corrandes, both in primary and secondary education. In addi-tion, in the last few years interschool meetings have been organized in various towns and cities around

6. For further information about this process of revitalization, see earlier studies like Casals and Sabater (2014) and Casals (2009).

7. A division of the Department of Education of the Catalan gov-ernment (Generalitat) responsible for promoting Catalan immer-sion and use.

Catalonia, with more expected to join the initiative in the near future.[8]

Two important particularities stand out in the process of implementation in schools as compared to other noteworthy experiences (in the Basque Country and Mallorca, for example): the initiative has come from the field of music; and most of the projects are based on empowering teachers for the educational use of corrandes. The key points and main aspects of the project in Catalonia are as follows:

The reasoning behind the use of corrandes at school is pedagogical; it is based on their immense educational potential (in the areas of language, music, theater, attitudes, and so on). In other words, the intention is not to preserve or extend a taste for improvised poetry in Catalan, nor are there any other possible intentions, although obviously one thing influences another. This is not an end in itself but rather the consequence of an educational approach that aims to work more effectively on communication as a competency.

The goal is that students, each at their own level, are initiated into the art of improvisation. It is not just a question of introducing them to corrandes but rather of challenging them to become corrandistes themselves and daring them to improvise in public.

---

8. Apart from the *Corrandescola* project, other schemes and projects have existed in Catalonia and more and more are being designed, although many of them are proposals developed by a sole teacher.

It was decided to empower the teachers and more specifically those working in two subject areas (Catalan and music). Those working on oral improvisation in classrooms are teachers who have received specific training. In short, this is not a case of corrandistes with didactic training but rather teachers with notions of improvisation, who can teach how to improvise verses. This guarantees a satisfactory didactic approach and facilitates the inclusion of the Corrandescola program in the curriculum and the school education agenda. At any rate, the participation of well-known corrandistes at some point in the program is important, because they serve as a role model.

Given the area under discussion of this chapter, I will leave aside the specific aspects of the program (which can be consulted in Casals 2010) to focus on the results and benefits that have been identified. The research and pilot experiments show important benefits in different areas, these being especially remarkable in a type of student not used to playing a positive role in the classroom.

The work based on corrandes goes beyond the usual disciplinary compartmentalization of education: its focus is holistic and competency-based, in line with the latest, most innovative educational trends. It should be noted that the main teaching goal of this activity is to improve the competency of oral communication: being better prepared to reach the other using the sum of the available expressive resources (verbal, musical, and corporal). Accordingly, what is really appreciated and evaluated is communicative effectiveness, above and beyond syntactic, lexical, or melodic accuracy: whether students are able to obtain an adequate response, and whether they know how to respond to a particular challenge.

As a consequence, the work with corrandes is wholly interdisciplinary and has repercussions in different subject areas, such as the Catalan language in particular. In language and literature, most students show significant progress in terms of oral expression, vocabulary acquisition, and comprehension of and interest in poetry (see Casals 2011, 2012). And it has an impact on multiple aspects ranging from the argumentation and synthesis of ideas to the structuring of discourse and use of rhetorical devices. And despite being a purely oral activity, some improvement has even been detected in writing skills: for example, overcoming problems with placing the accent on words (stress) as a consequence of better identifying the separation of syllables and the accented syllable.

On the other hand, it should not be forgotten that the work with corrandes also has a very positive impact on music education and different types of transversal learning (learning that transcends the curricular subjects). This can be summed up as follows:

Benefits are seen in music in aspects such as solo singing (Casals, Vilar, and Ayats 2011), making singing come naturally, expressiveness in sung performance, and the signification of tradition (Casals, Ayats, and Vilar 2010).

In drama teaching, there are positive results as regards the ability to act in public, with more expressive use of the body and better modulation of the voice.

In terms of interpersonal relationships and personal growth, students are forced to challenge themselves, face up to and deal with mistakes, overcome shyness, and express and cope with criticism, among other things.

Complementarily, another reason for the success of the Corrandescola program, apart from improved academic performance, is that it offers students resources to help cope with difficulties and challenges at school. Two of them deserve special mention: the program provides tools for guiding teaching-learning processes in the fields of oral expression, poetry, theater, and creativity; and it helps to rethink and renew the organization of school festivals.

Corrandes and the Emotional Bond with the Language

Holding a conversation through singing and doing so playfully in a group is a positive experience with a high emotional impact. And this is precisely the greatest contribution that the corrandes—or any linguistic activity—can make to the survival of a language, in this case Catalan. In fact, some authors do not hesitate to claim that "positive attitudes toward the language and the desire to do things with people who speak it are two decisive factors for its acquisition" (Vila, Siqués, and Oller 2009, 120). And naturally this is a crucial point when considering non-Catalan-speaking contexts—in which experiences associated with Catalan are few and not always positive—or contexts in which there is reticence toward Catalan or open rejection.

In the case of pilot experiments carried out in centers with a low or non-existent percentage of Catalan speakers, we have seen students with little or no interest in learning Catalan, or insecure about using it, become motivated and end up having fun in Catalan. And although this may seem paradoxical, the use of a communicative device that requires so many skills at the same time in initial learning environments is not a problem. The motivating, ludic character of corrandes, the ease with which the activity and its mechanisms can be adapted to any level, the impossibility of constant correction by the teacher, and the implicit normalization of error are some of the explanatory factors.

It is interesting to note that when non-Catalan speaking students cannot find any reference similar to the corrandes in their mother tongue, they quickly accept that this activity (conversing playfully through singing) has to be in Catalan; they do not contemplate the possibility of doing so in another language. On the other hand, the experience of rap in Catalan in some schools, in which students have references in English and Spanish, has met with much more interference between languages.

The recreational and social use of Catalan not only helps to raise interest in using it and, ultimately, in learning it; it also leads to greater social cohesion. Seeing as corrandes are conversations that stem from their interests and opinions, the class group builds up more relationships among its members, they get to know each other better, and a sense of group identity emerges.

By Way of a Conclusion

In view of the research and results obtained in the ten years since the launch of the first project, which systematized and laid the foundations for the use of corrandes in schools (the Corrandescola program), it is possible to talk about a pedagogical success story and ambitious perspectives for the future. Among other things, the results reveal the potential of corrandes in terms of experiencing Catalan, of its use and, ultimately, its survival. Because for a language to survive and advance—and even more so in the case of one with fewer speakers and without the backing of a state—it is imperative that potential speakers build emotional bonds and associate positive experiences with that language, and discover spaces in which it is necessary, functional, and useful. The use of corrandes in schools has the capacity to meet all these demands.

In the same vein, only if people are able to live out their whole lives using a language (from shopping and browsing the Internet to defending themselves in court, making declarations of love, or insulting each other) is it possible to imagine a future for that language, encouraging those whose mother tongue it is and attracting new speakers. And as can be deduced from the data presented at the beginning, the world of leisure (cinema, television, music, and so on) is one of the spaces in which Catalan is fighting a non-stop battle for its future. It is a space in which corrandes, by way of being a recreational artistic activity, and as a form of entertainment, can also help to confirm and to show in certain contexts just how much fun it is possible to have in Catalan too.

Bibliography

Ayats, Jaume. 2007. *Les chants traditionnels des pays catalans*. Cahiers d'ethnomusicologie régionale 8. Toulouse: Isatis.

Casals, Albert. 2009. "La cançó amb text improvisat: Disseny i experimentació d'una proposta interdisciplinària per a Primària." PhD diss., Autonomous University of Barcelona. At http:// www.tdx.cat/TDX-0324110-114328 (accessed February 2, 2017).

———, ed. 2009. *Corrandescola: proposta didàctica per treballar la glosa a l'escola*. Cerdanyola del Vallès: ICE-UAB.

———. 2011. "Canta i et diré com t'expresses." *Articles de Didàctica de la Llengua i la Literatura 54 (Spring)*: 37–44.

———. 2012. "Corrandescola: del cant a la improvisació poètica." *Temps d'Educació* 42 (Winter): 111–30.

Casals, Albert, and Maria Dolors Sabater. 2014. "Glosar: una activitat pedagògica i lúdica." Paper presented at the IV Simposi Internacional sobre l'Ensenyament del Català, Vic, Catalonia, Spain, April.

Casals, Albert, Jaume Ayats, and Mercè Vilar. 2010. "Improvised Song in Schools: Breaking Away from the Perception of Traditional Song as Infantile by Introducing a Traditional Adult Practice." *Oral Tradition* 25, no.2 (October): 365–80. At http://

journal.oraltradition.org/issues/25ii/casals (accessed February 2, 2017).

Casals, Albert, Mercè Vilar, and Jaume Ayats. 2011. " 'I'm not sure if I can . . . but I want to sing!' Research on Singing as a Soloist through the Art of Improvising Verses." *British Journal of Music Education* 28, no.3 (November): 247–61.

Frechina, Josep Vicent. 2014. *Pensar en vers. La cançó improvisada als països de la Mediterrània.* Calaceit: Llibres de Caramella.

Gross, Joan. 2008. "Defendiendo la (agri)cultura: Reterritorializing Culture in the Puerto Rican Décima." *Oral Tradition* 23, no.2 (October): 219–34. At http://journal.oraltradition.org/issues/23ii/gross (accessed February 2, 2017).

Ionita, Cristian. 2017. "The Catalan Question: From Charlemagne to Puigdemont." *The World on the Map.* At https://www.edmaps.com/html/catalonia_in_seven_maps.html (accessed February 10, 2017).

Lanz, Tilman. 2016. "Minority Cosmopolitanism: The Catalan Independence Process, the EU, and the Framework Convention for National Minorities." *Journal on Ethnopolitics and Minority Issues in Europe* 15: 31–58.

Plataforma per la Llengua. 2016. *InformeCAT 2016: 50 dades sobre la llengua catalana.* Barcelona: Plataforma per la Llengua; Barcelona. At https://www.plataforma-llengua.cat/que-fem/estudis-i-publicacions/173/informecat-2016 (accessed February 2, 2017).

Pujol, Josep Maria. 1985. "Literatura tradicional i etnopoètica: balanç d'un folklorist." In *La cultura popular a debat*, edited by Dolors Llopart, Joan Prat, and Llorenç Prats. Barcelona: Alta Fulla; Fundació Serveis de Cultura Popular.

Serrà, Antoni. 2005. "Funció del glosador en la societat preindustrial." In *Formes d'expressió oral*, edited by Felip Munar. Manacor: Consell de Mallorca; Associació Cultural Es Canonge de Santa Cirga.

Vallverdú, Francesc. 1984. "A Sociolinguistic History of Catalan." *International Journal of the Sociology of Language* 47 (January): 13–28.

Vila, Ignasi, Carina Siqués, and Judith Oller. 2009. "Usos lingüístics de l'alumnat d'origen estranger a l'educació primària de Catalunya." *Zeitschrift für Katalanistik / Revista d'Estudis Catalans* 22: 95–124. At http://www.romanistik.uni-freiburg. de/pusch/zfk/cat/2009.htm (accessed February 2, 2017).

White, Linda. 2001. "Orality and Basque Nationalism: Dancing with the Devil or Waltzing into the Future?" *Oral Tradition* 16, no.1 (March): 3–28. At http://journal.oraltradition.org/issues/16i/ white (accessed February 2, 2017).

Xarxa CRUSCAT. 2015. *VIII Informe sobre la situació de la llengua catalana (2014)*. Barcelona: Observatori de la Llengua Catalana. At http:// blogs.iec.cat/cruscat/publicacions/informe/ (accessed February 2, 2017).

6

El Punto: Forms of Transmission in Cuba—Knowledge and Meanings Connected With Everyday Practice

Patricia Tápanes Suárez

Guajira, Improvisada, Sentimental, Octosilábica, and *Fugaz* are all names for improvised Cuban poetry, *Punto.* Poetry whose fleeting, forgotten nature turns everything around it into magic and, on occasions, moves far away from the world of the rational.

Cuban peasants' poetry, singing, and musical accompaniment; *Tonada* on top of which rehearsed or improvised verses are sung; each verse has ten lines and a precise, octosyllabic meter termed *Décima.* It is accompanied by plucked string instruments (lute, *tres,* guitar and, sometimes, double-bass), with optional idiophone accompaniment (usually clave, guiro, and/or marimba), and membraphones (bongo, conga).

Musicological research has demonstrated that a nation's music contains the solid, indelible characteristics of its experiences, history, and traditions: "They come together, to a greater or lesser extent, with other factors that, in turn, are determined by heterogeneous social spheres meaning, consequently, that there may be great contrasts and nuances between musical tones in different urban, suburban, and rural areas to the extent to which there are mutual influences between these spheres, as well as external influences" (Pérez Cassola 2008, PAGE).

Music of Hispanic origin was strongly protected from external influences in peasant society. In the first place, and as the most common stylistic feature, it included the sound of plucked strings, using imported instruments (such as guitars, bandurrias, tiples, and lutes) and original Cuban instruments (such as the tres); second, it retained the Décima meter, the Cubans' favorite form of poetry and, as Samuel Feijoo put it, "the perfect spiritual form of Cuban music, the most loved by the people." The Décima meter has always been the form chosen for songs, becoming the essentially national form, with great beauty and a very particular, natural style (Pérez Cassola 2008).

In our country we make music using styles taken from previous cultures. From the island's first poetic echoes onward, the improvised Guajira Décima has always been there in the special Tonadas, the rhythms and sounds that made it possible to write our highly extensive popular songbook, and without having taken any other musical or poetic form into account until the present day.

There are interesting characteristics such as Gautequ', Canturia, and Parranda, and these are the places where you can see the main variations in Punto: the Punto Libre (in which there is a free meter in the Tonadas), the Punto Fijo, which includes

Clave (with a strict meter in the Tonadas), and the Cruzado (in which the stress moves in syncopation depending on the accompanying music's tempo). Punto Pinareño or Vueltabajero, Espirituano, and Camagüeyano are among the other options.

"Al cantío de un gallo" (To a rooster's crow) is a common expression in Cuban Guajiro when a party is getting together: dance, music, food, and drink are the preamble for improvised singing; between two and four pairs of improvising poets come together, and their dialogues capture the attention of those of us who are hypnotized after listening to them for just a few seconds, the explosion of an octosyllabic verse, with a set rhythm and ten well-linked verses. The Décima— or "Sentimental Guajira," as some poets call it—goes right into you, makes each poet's and the spectator's hair stand on end, and the oral game begins.

There are different types of stages; improvising poets always feel the need to sing whenever they hear the sound of the lute, the tres, or the guitar. In the past, the doorway to a wine cellar could be the ideal place; a patio inside a building; the cool shade of a good tree. Nowadays, although some of the traditional stages are still used, the improvised Décima has spread out to larger areas such as squares, theaters, beach bars, and public events. But there can be no doubt that Cuban minstrels feel most at home in more peasant-style surroundings, where the pressure of modern life does not affect them, and they can play with time.

Madruga, Güines, Ceiba Mocha, Güira de Melena, Limonar, and Las Tunas: all of these towns

and places on our island have been conscious or unconscious witnesses to a unique, unrepeatable act;
entertainment that, without any apparent preparation, moves even the most sophisticated of audiences. Occasions vary from birthday celebrations,
casual parties, family meals, poetry encounters,
planned singing sessions, and festivals to just spontaneous singing.

An afternoon spent anywhere in Cuba, under a
Balsa tree at a beach bar provides shade for more
than three hundred people, most of them men of
different ages and social classes; incredible amounts
of rum are often drunk, there is a lot of smoking,
and loud talking about what they are going to hear.
Several improvising poets begin to appear; members
of the audience, friends, and admirers, start greeting
each other; the musicians tune up; pairs are named,
and the peasant party kicks off. Improvising bards
stop time with their songs, forming part of a scene
in which the audience, under the spell of the songs,
adopts a certain attitude; so there is real communication. But the poets also use Décima as verse, and the
music as accompaniment, and adopt other people's
attitudes at the same time as influencing them.

And there they are, you see them getting onto
the stage, or just taking their place in front of the
musicians, who sit on stools or stand, and start the
concert. The strings paint over the silence and the
noise of the crowd, and the color of Punto Libre,
blessed in its feet-tapping origins, gives the poets the
freedom to sing without any music-imposed obligations. It is then that an invisible process begins in the

improvising poets' minds, an incredible ability that involves everybody participating, and in which time, mood, the audience's acceptance, the context, and that daring girl called Muse are all essential.

After half an hour of singing, the atmosphere is different. Depending on the subject that the improvising poets take on, the surfeit of alcoholic beverages and local preferences for particular poets can call for a change of tone. The cultural meaning of improvised poetry turns around and becomes highly social and symbolic. The dialogue between the poets can become a moment of relaxation from the pressure of daily life, a moment for laughter; but it can also become aggressive, with conflict, offence, misunderstandings, and even desperation. As you watch them improvise, you see them put their characters together step by step, using their knowledge and memories to improvise, and, above all, living through their characters; and, by manipulating the ritual, seeking the acceptance of everybody listening.

Weddings are always celebrated by playing string instruments such as the lute, the tres, and the guitar, although other instruments—such as güiros, claves, and bongos—are sometimes used too, usually to provide rhythm to back the strings up. Some Cuban improvising poets speak their improvisations, either as an exercise or to entertain, but that is not the usual way in our country: it is sung improvisation that is of sociocultural importance.

The instrumentalists, who are an indispensable part of the improvising poetry performance, use Cuban or Guajiro Punto as a musical form, hardly changing its original form, the musicians only being differentiated in terms of each player's speed and skill. The lute is played to mark all the beginnings and ends of the musical interludes; the tres and the guitar are musical backing.

Oral tradition is passed on from generation to generation mimetically, and continually recreated by the groups who make use of it. People who pass Punto on vary from children to old people, illiterate people to graduates, with no distinction between phenotypes, genders, or religions. The society I belong to holds it to be an indispensable spiritual and a cultural activity that is of great heritage value. It is present in our everyday lives, at family, social, civic, festival meetings, in our homes, in local squares, and in public buildings, which also become places for extending it for each of us to use it in a free, spontaneous way.

At performances (singing sessions, parties, festivals, and competitions) organized by promoters and institutions with responsibility for protecting and promoting the genre, instrumentalists, improvising poets, and performers appear in front of varied audiences. The organizers of these acts vary depending on whether the events are public or private, although, in general, they tend to be the local promoters in each place, civil servants at public institutions, or other groups connected with the genre.

With no academy to offer systematic learning, it has always been passed on from one generation to the next. In many cases it is passed on within the family, and in close connection with the local area;

in others, however, it is learned mimetically by listening, observing, repeating, getting involved in the process of formal education, and enriching it by putting it into practice.

One method has emerged from the wish to protect collective memory, historical and cultural signs of identity, and it combines traditional oral transmission with a program or workshop for children that is taught by Punto performers. The methods followed are entertaining. It was put together by Alexis Díaz Pimienta and is taught at cultural centers and schools throughout Cuba. Décima rules are taught, as are techniques for improvisation and the melodies that are sung, as well as the playing of instruments that accompany Punto. Other manuals have been added to poet Alexis Diaz's methods, methodology programs and suggestions from other performers in the genre that take into account the different characteristics of different regions in Cuba and the diversity of the tradition on the island.

Instrumentalists learn techniques for playing their instruments in two different ways: teaching themselves by copying and playing with musicians from this tradition at different events and in different activities, and at music schools around the country.

The performers, Tonadistas, poets, and Parranderos use Punto to address different subjects individually and collectively (love, death, hope, nature), subjects that illustrate events and experiences from everyday life.

All Cuban peasants consider it to be cultural heritage of great value, true to its characteristics, and one that makes use of those features depending on what each performer in the genre needs to express. People respect and admire performers and they, in turn, respect and follow the ways and means of those who went before them and have an important place in the tradition. Values are passed on at performances and creativity is encouraged, as is pleasure in the genre for both the performers and the general public.

As Abel Zabala (2007, PAGE) puts it: "This is a very old art form . . . An art form with its roots in prehistory . . . Ageless music with no frontiers, which has reached the present day and continues to cross centuries and cultures."

And it was then that the poet "dared to address natural phenomena and, at first, called himself a priest in order preserve his vocabulary. Which is why in modern times poets are invested in the street, by the public, in order to defend their poetry. Nowadays, too, poets are the oldest priesthood. They used to have pacts with darkness, and now they have to interpret the light" (Neruda 1974, 361).

We like to imagine that our 'Guajira Sentimental' –elegant, anonymous, and fleeting– is moving toward that light.

Bibliography

Pérez Cassola, Sonia Margarita. 2008. Album notes on CD. Various Artists, *Soy la décima guajira*. Havana: Egrem.

Zabala, Abel. 2007. *Al son de la rústica cuerda. El verso improvisado en el Río de la Plata*. Granada: Fundación El Marchal.

7

A Strategy to Produce Your Own Cultural Ecosystem: The Case of *Bertsolaritza*

*Harkaitz Zubiri, Xabier Aierdi, and
Alfredo Retortillo*

Too Long to Be a Mere Fad

What makes *bertsolaritza* (the art of improvised verse singing in the Basque language) something more than just a quaint, folkloric appendage to Basque culture? After all, in a world that is becoming progressively more globalized and commercialized, the potential target audience for improvised verse singing, which is based on an age-old tradition, is a mere drop in the vast ocean of cultural consumers. Furthermore, in the cultural field, languages such as Spanish, English, and French are hegemonic, even in the only region in which the Basque language is spoken, and to make matters worse, the original

Several researchers participated in this project, either in the first or second phase or in both: Xabier Aierdi, Juan Aldaz, Eider Alkorta, Alfredo Retortillo, and Harkaitz Zubiri. We would like to thank the Bertsozale Elkartea and Mintzola for asking us to conduct this piece of research. We are also grateful to the volunteers who passed out the questionnaires and to those who participated in our in-depth interviews; their time and generosity is greatly appreciated.

habitat of *bertsolaritza,* namely rural society, has disappeared. Inertia has therefore long been driving *bertsolaritza* toward extinction.

Table 7.1. Basque population cultural practices

	Music	Books	Cinema	Concerts	Theater	Bertsolaritza
Basque citizens in any language	69.9	58	54.8	38.2	21.9	7.6
Basque citizens in Basque	46.4	6.3	0.3	8	5.4	7.6
Basque speakers in any language	72.6	57.5	54.7	46.5	24.7	17.3
Basque speakers in Basque	68.8	20.7	1.02	16	12.5	17.3

However, the number of *bertsolaritza* followers today shows that currently, the art is as successful as other cultural disciplines in the same language, a circumstance that is not at all common in other contexts. Data from the Basque Observatory of Culture (table 7.1) suggests that the percentage of the population who attend *bertsolaritza* events (17.3 percent said they attended a session at least once a year) is similar to those percentages reported by other cultural disciplines: reading books in free time (20.7 percent at least once in the last three months), going to music concerts (16.0 percent at least once a year), or going to the theater (12.5 percent at least once a year) (Zubiri 2010, 2014). Nevertheless, it should be noted that, as with other cultural disciplines in the Basque language, the frequency with which people go to *bertsolaritza* events is well below that of cultural disciplines in Spanish and French. This is true even among Basque bilinguals in the region in which Basque is spoken.

It has often been remarked upon that 14,000 people gather every four years in the Bilbao Exhibition Centre to attend the final of the Basque Oral Poetry Championship, as John Miles Foley called it. This event is broadcast live on public television and averages around 100,000 viewers, a figure which shoots up to 200,000 during the highpoints of the contest. It helps to read Foley's (2007) description of the final, because the event is too familiar for us and we often forget just how striking it is to see so many people sitting there, almost from dawn till dusk with only a short lunch break, listening to improvised verses composed in accordance with specific metrics and rhymes and sung *a capella*, either individually or in pairs. It is still more remarkable if we take into account that these audience and viewer numbers, 14,000 and 100,000, are uncommon in this context. While it is true that, on their forthcoming tour, the US hard rock band Guns N' Roses will most likely attract even larger audiences at their concerts, given the demographics of the Basque Country this is not a common occurrence. The region has just three million inhabitants and less than 800,000 Basque speakers. Furthermore, although no official research has been conducted on this subject, the data offered by the media covering cultural events reveals that over the last twenty-five years only eleven musicians or bands have attracted audiences significantly larger than that recorded for the Bertsolaritza Championship: Pink Floyd (1994), the San Sebastian Choral Society (1997), Luciano Pavarotti (1998), The Rolling Stones (2003, 2007), U2 (2005, 2010), Depeche Mode

(2006), Bob Dylan (2006), Bruce Springsteen (2008, 2009, 2011, 2012, 2016), ACDC (2010), Bon Jovi (2011), and Shakira (2011). Of those, four attracted more than 20,000 people and seven had audiences of over 30,000. The performers were English, Irish, North American, Australian, and Colombian, with the San Sebastian Choral Society being the only one from the Basque Country.

But *bertsolaritza* is not just a *happening* that takes place once every four years. While it is evident that the Championship is essential in social and media terms, due to the exposure it provides the art, in quantitative terms (that is, audiences) the Championship is not really all that significant in comparison with the *bertsolaritza* events that take place all year round (Figure 7.1). For instance, in 2013, a total of 30,245 people went to one of the various Championship events, whereas 263,884 people went to other *bertsolaritza* events (when interpreting these specific figures, it should be noted that they do not reflect individual people but rather the number of tickets sold). In other words, the audience at the Championship represented only 10 percent of all those who attended *bertsolaritza* events throughout the course of the whole year (Xenpelar Dokumentazio Zentroa 2016).

According to Aierdi et al. (2007), *bertsolaritza* has a noteworthy number of devotees: 14 percent of Basque speakers love *bertsolaritza*, 26 percent like it, 29 percent like it moderately, and only 32 percent do not like it at all. If, in order to avoid the bias of political correctness (because loving *bertsolaritza* may be

Figure 7.1. Public all year long and in the
Championship (2013)

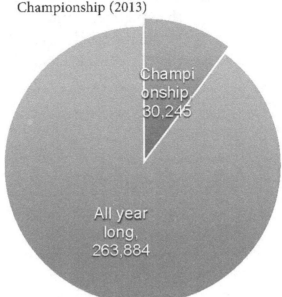

considered politically correct by many people in the
Basque Country), we assume that only those who
claim to love *bertsolaritza* can be considered devotees, then we can conclude that there are over 100,000
bertsolaritza enthusiasts in a language community of
800,000 people. The data from the Championship final suggests that there are, in fact, more than 100,000
devotees, because otherwise how can you explain the
fact that 100,000 Basque speakers watched the event
on television and 14,000 attended it live? Aierdi et
al. (2007) also offer some other interesting facts:
60 percent of Basque speakers knew who the current champion was, suggesting that it is a broader
cultural phenomenon that does not just interest the

art's most ardent followers. Moreover, 60.1 percent of those who claimed to moderately like *bertsolaritza* knew who the champion was, and 43.8 percent of those who said they did not like *bertsolaritza* at all were also in possession of this knowledge.

A New Habitat

The data we have shown so far is quite recent, that is, it is from a period in which the original habitat of *bertsolaritza*, namely rural society, no longer exists. Nowadays, six out of ten (62 percent) Basque citizens and six out of ten (60 percent) Basque speakers live in capital cities and their conurbations, and 43 percent of *bertsolaritza* events take place in those urban areas. Two conclusions can be drawn from these figures, one that is obvious and one that is incorrect:

Table 7.2. Population, Basque speakers, and *Bertsolaritza* Events in Capital Cities and their Conurbations (CCC)

	Population	Basque speakers in the Basque Country	*Bertsolaritza* events in the Basque Country	Basque speakers in each CCC	Basque speakers in each CCC as a percentage of the total number of Basque speakers in each province	*Bertsolaritza* events in each CCC as a percentage of the total number of *bertsolaritza* events in each province
CCC	62%	60%	43%	-	-	-
Bilbao CCC	29%	27%	11%	24%	75%	57%
Donostia-San Sebastián-Irun CCC	10%	21%	17%	42%	46%	35%
Vitoria-Gasteiz	8%	7%	4%	24%	95%	38%
Pamplona-Iruñea CCC	10%	4%	10*%	8%	40%	93*%
Baiona-Angelu-Biarritz	4%	1%	0.3%	7%	14%	5%

Source: Data from the INE, INSEE, Aztiker, and Bapatean 2014.
Note: the percentage of bertsolaritza events held in the Pamplona-Iruñea CCC is somewhat misleading, because it does not correspond to the conurbation itself but rather to the so-called Merindad (county), which covers a much larger area.

first, that *bertsolaritza* now forms part of the cultural environment in the Basque Country's capital cities and their conurbations, and second, that most *bertsolaritza* events still take place in rural areas. As stated earlier, however, this second conclusion is erroneous because although a few areas outside the main cities still retain their eminently "rural" natures, this is not always (or even mostly) the case. Agriculture was predominant until it started to decline with the onset of the industrial revolution; then in the 1980s the service sector increased, industry decreased, and agriculture became almost insignificant (in 2001 it represented only 3 percent of the Basque economy). Consequently, most formerly rural areas can no longer be considered "rural" at all.

Bertsolaritza Becomes a Social Movement

So why has *bertsolaritza* not died out? There are several reasons, but we believe that the social project established by this age-old art form is an essential piece of the puzzle. In social terms, *bertsolaritza* became an art-based social movement in the 1980s. Our analysis is wholly consistent with Jon Sarasua's (Sarasua 2004, 2007, 2013; Garzia, Sarasua, and Egaña 2001a, 2001b) concept of self-constitution: Sarasua states that at some point in its evolution *bertsolaritza* became an organized movement with a sociocultural strategy. This is also the basis of our argument, but when a group of people organize themselves, they can do so in a number of different ways, and in our opinion, *bertsolaritza* self-constituted as a social movement. This metamorphosis increased *bertsolaritza*'s capacity to generate its own cultural ecosystem, and consequently, it became better able to promote the quantitative and qualitative growth of its own practitioners (known as *bertsolari*s in the Basque language), supporters and followers.[1]

There are several ways of defining a social movement. According to the behaviorist perspective on collective conduct (Turner and Killian 1987), social movements are irrational and contagious, and only spread under pressure. Mobilization theory and political process theory, on the other hand, hold that social movements take advantage of a window of opportunity to organize themselves and confront structural problems (Zald and Ash 1966; Gamson 1975; McCarthy and Zald 1977; Tilly 1978; MacAdam 1982; Polleta and Jasper 2001; Rao, Morrill, and Zald 2000). Therefore, according to this perspective, it is not irrationality but rather rationality that is at the core of social movements (Garner in Garner and Zald, 2012).

The latter perspective has been criticized because power is depicted as being monopolized by just one pole, the importance of culture (understood in the broadest sense of the term) is underestimated, and, consequently, it seems that social movements exclusively aim to influence states (Armstrong and Bernstein 2008). Likewise, it has also been criticized for overestimating rationality and taking for granted

---

1. The term "supporters" is used here to refer to those people who make an active effort to help organize events and run verse schools; "followers" is used to denote those who simply attend events and contests.

the preexistence of a collective actor (Polleta and Jasper 2001).

The New Social Movement Theory (NSMT) takes a different perspective: social movements are created in the context of macro-historic transformations, but they do not automatically derive from the needs related to those changes, because they must be pushed by social actors to become autonomous subjects and so change their situation (Offe 1985; Touraine 1981, 1985, 2004; Melucci 1985, 1989, 1996). Based on examples such as the feminist, gay, green, and pro-peace movements, the NSMT states that social movements are defined by conflicts; however, the theory also claims that there is no central conflict and that the main aim of social movements is not necessarily to influence political authorities, but rather to achieve recognition as a social actor and change the cultural model. This is something social movements have indeed attempted to do in several fields: territory, way of life, body, health, sexual identity, commercialization of social life, cultural and linguistic heritage and cultural habits, among others (Offe 1985; Mouffe 1984). Nevertheless, all social movements have to deal with the new global order, the so-called one-dimensional globalization, and all are actors in what Touraine defines as the *grand refus,* albeit from different positions, perspectives, and starting points. Moreover, all tend to become progressively more informational, giving priority to communication while at the same time following the May '68 tradition of *l'action exemplaire,* striving to engage in spectacular actions in order to raise public awareness (Castells

1997, 2015). The research conducted within the Northern Basque Country's Seaska education project (Heidemann 2012, 2014) and the social movements that joined forces to demand television channels for certain minoritized European languages (Hourigan 2001) were based on the NSMT.

The *Bertsolaritza* Social Movement

Identity, Conflict, Antagonists, and Aims

The *Bertsolaritza* social movement (from here on the BSM) defines itself as an autonomous cultural project. Other cultural disciplines (music, literature, theater, and so on) in the Basque Country had the option of importing international models, because they were better-known. *Bertsolaritza*, on the other hand, had no chance of adapting an international model to fit its own individual situation, because although examples of improvised verse singing do exist in countries such as Brazil, the United States, Cuba, and Spain, they were neither visible nor well-known in the Basque Country at the time when the the BSM was emerging. Therefore, when some practitioners and supporters of *bertsolaritza* decided to organize themselves in order to guarantee the survival of the art, they had no choice but to create a new model. Several proposals were tabled, including setting up a company to manage a traveling *bertsolaritza* contest-show and creating an association charged with managing practitioners' careers. When those who were active in the BSM are asked to explain how the movement emerged, two key moments are often mentioned in relation to that critical time: the setting up of the verse schools (special schools dedicated to teaching the art of *bertsolaritza*) and the establishment of the *Bertsozale Elkartea* (the Association of Friends of *Bertsolaritza*). However, these were not decisions made by any one person at any one specific moment in time and although the establishment of the Association of Friends of *Bertsolaritza* was hugely important, the BSM had gradually been gaining momentum for a long time beforehand. The whole process began before the association was created, and besides, the emergence of the BSM had always been based mainly on the local work carried out in each city, town, or village.

Words as different as *culture* and *autonomous* seem synonymous when pronounced by the BSM, because being autonomous from other agents has notably been the cornerstone of the BSM's self-definition: the BSM has always claimed its independence from political parties, public institutions, and other agents.

As culture became progressively more globalized and commercialized, agents working in the field of *bertsolaritza* asked themselves how they should react to the new context (Sarasua 2004), the answer being: by becoming a social movement. The question, however, is an ongoing one and reveals the conflictive context in which the movement has always found itself. Culture in languages other than Basque and commercial culture are its antagonists. In other words, the BSM opposes trends that destroy cultural heritage and diversity, which is why it competes with those *others* in order to dispute their cultural hegemony. The BSM explicitly uses ecological discourse (Garzia 2007; Sarasua 2013), in the sense that caring for and revitalizing cultural heritage means fostering existing diversity, and for this to happen the BSM believes it is necessary to create conditions conducive to promoting and expanding *bertsolaritza*.

The main aim is to guarantee the survival of an art form, which is why the BSM invests in a social strategy, because it believes that adequate social conditions will necessarily provide *bertsolaritza* with more opportunities to strengthen and grow.

The method employed to this end is to invest mainly in the social project and to leave the artistic side of things to practitioners. This strategy is fairly uncommon, although there are many cases of the opposite approach being taken, with movements striving to influence an art by directly conditioning artistic practice, usually by creating guidelines for artists and practitioners. Such cases are well-known in literature, for instance. However, the BSM has always followed the criterion of non-intervention in artistic matters, stating instead its determination to invest in measures designed to foster sociocultural transformation.

The priority is not to influence a powerful agent such as the state (although the BSM does not completely ignore this path), but rather to mobilize practitioners, active supporters and actual and potential followers. This approach explains the creation of the verse schools, associations, and championships, the establishment of media policies, and, above all, *bertsolaritza's action examplaire*, known as *bert-so-saioa*, the *bertsolaritza* event in which practitioners improvise their verses in front of an audience.

Basically, the BSM is oriented toward cultural transformation, with culture being understood as art, but also as something broader. In a context of cultural globalization, the BSM takes an art form as its reference and creates a social movement around it. Individuality and even isolation are not uncommon in the arts. There may be many small-scale, introspective, competitive lobbies, but few have the will or the means to effect true collective or social transformation. Yet the BSM emerged and expanded in a different way. Integrating practitioners, supporters, and followers into an autonomous, collective agent was quite an innovation, particularly since the strategy aimed to produce the social conditions required for the art to flourish and grow.

Figure 7.2. Number of bertsolaritza events (1990–2015)

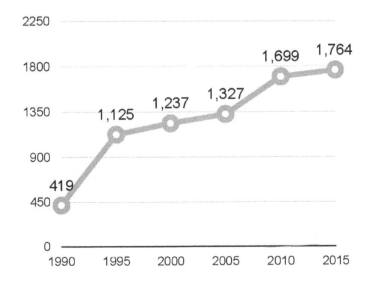

If we analyze the increase recorded in the number of events, practitioners, and spectators, it becomes evident that the BSM is achieving its initial goals.

The number of events has increased steadily over the last twenty-five years (figure 7.2): 419 events took place in 1990, 1,125 in 1995, 1,237 in 2000, 1,327 in 2005, 1,699 in 2010, and 1,764 in 2015. Therefore, the BSM's most visible manifestation, the *bertso saioa*, the principal symbol of this art form, has become more popular than ever.

The number of practitioners has also risen over the last twenty-five years (figure 7.3): whereas in 1990 there were only 290 *bertsolaris*, after a steady and prolonged increase, the figure in 2015 was 859.

Figure 7.3. Number of bertsolaris (1990–2015)

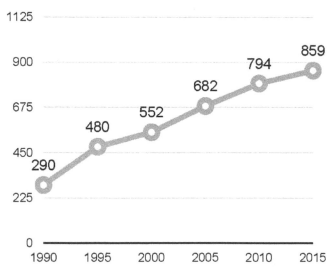

Audience numbers also confirm the hypothesis of the growth brought about by the BSM (figure 7.4). During the so-called *boom* that occurred in *bertsolaritza* between 1990 and 1995, around 223,924 people attended *bertsolaritza* events every year. This number dropped to around 160,000 over the following years (we will explain this decline later) and then bounced back even higher, with figures of around 260,000 per year being recorded over the most recent period.

Figure 7.4. Attendance at bertsolari events (1990–2015)

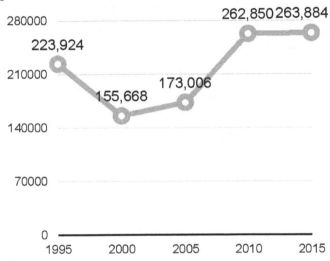

The growth in audience numbers was not just quantitative, but qualitative as well. Some decades ago, the public at *bertsolaritza* events was more homogenous. Then, during the period in which the BSM emerged, audiences started to "splinter," as Garzia (2000) puts it, becoming much more heterogeneous than ever before. Garzia states that in the pre-*boom* period, *bertsolaris* sung to the "people" rather than to their actual audiences, just as they used to during the era of resistance to Franco's dictatorship, but that over recent years, audiences have become more varied. Garzia (2012) defines the current period as multipolar, and indeed, from the year 2000 onward, audiences have become increasingly diverse and complex.

Nowadays, total audience numbers are higher, but audiences are different from those in the *boom* period because the underlying growth model is different as well. Today, there are a greater number of smaller events, as opposed to the large-scale events of the past that were only attended by a certain ideological segment of the population. This means that there is more variety, since depending on its specific characteristics, each event will attract a different type of public. What we are witnessing today may well be the beginning of a diversification *boom*.

One of the characteristics of today's *bertsolaritza* events is that they attract different types of people in terms of age and cultural tastes, for example. However, this new multipolar period raises new questions such as how to make events general enough to appeal to a heterogeneous, ever-more-diverse audience, while at the same time catering to their increasingly specialist tastes. The strategy for hegemonic articulation may prove useful for the current period (Laclau and Mouffe 1985, Laclau 2005).

Link to its Specific Moment in History

The emergence of the BSM is evidently related to the specific moment in history in which it occurred. *Bertsolaritza* used to be the dominant cultural discipline in Basque-speaking rural society, a cultural ecosystem in which it had few competitors. The transmission from one generation to the next occurred as part of an apparently *natural* process and there was no need for a conscious strategy. Society came into contact with *bertsolaritza* in the places in which it was practiced (cider houses, bars, private homes, and so on), and future practitioners learned the art as though learning were a spontaneous process.

Then that ecosystem disappeared. The places in which *bertsolaritza* was practiced were radically transformed and, almost overnight, those who had been the majority suddenly became a tiny minority. These changes threatened the very practice of *bertsolaritza*, putting both its visibility and its future into grave danger. This radical drop in status seems mainly to have been the consequence of a much broader set of historical processes, rather than changes within *bertsolaritza* itself. The Western world underwent an extreme process of urbanization and industrialization, followed by the decisive emergence of the third sector and, eventually, the dawning and expansion of the informational era (Castells 1997, 2015). Old spaces, jobs, and ways of life disappeared. *Bertsolaritza* was part of the old system, and as that model was eroded, inertia started pushing the art form toward the sidelines until it became a marginal cultural discipline, seemingly doomed to extinction.

During the twentieth century there were a number of attempts to revitalize *bertsolaritza*, but the emergence of the BSM in the 1980s proved by far the most effective means of coping with the problems of the new era. The BSM has created new

spaces for transmission, cultural associations to ar-
ticulate volunteer work, strategies geared toward
ensuring greater media impact, and new discourses
for defining the art of improvised verse singing (pi-
oneered by Xabier Amuriza). It has also promoted
massive public and media mobilization through the
Championships. Organized initiative proved the key
to the art form's survival and subsequent expansion
at the very moment at which inertia was pushing it
in the other direction.

While it is clear that the historic moment did not
inevitably or directly trigger the social movement,
and although it is true that there was no preexisting
collective initiative, it is equally true that the changes
themselves constituted obvious warning signals that
resulted in the wake-up call that kick-started the
whole process. It should be noted, however, that
other cultural disciplines also experienced similar
risks in the same context, and none of them reacted
by coming together to form a movement. Thus, at
a specific moment in history, in which there was
no preexisting collective initiative, the key to *bertsolaritza*'s survival was its organization of a social
movement.

Nonetheless, although *bertsolaritza* was revitalized, that does not mean it ever recovered the dominant position that it used to have in Basque rural
society. Times have changed completely. The Basque
language is now minoritized and endangered and
the influence of globalization has spread to the cultural field as well. Furthermore, cultural disciplines
are now much more diverse. As is the case nowadays

with all cultural manifestations, it is impossible for *bertsolaritza* to maintain the same level of importance it used to have for its devotees. Whereas in the past it was a two-way struggle between literature and cinema for the dominance of narrative, nowadays both disciplines have a multitude of other competitors, and the same is true for *bertsolaritza*. The cultural playing field is, in general, becoming much more diverse.

Organization and Resource Mobilization

Now, more than ever, *bertsolaritza* is a socialization network centered around improvised verse singing. This is a direct consequence of the work carried out by the BSM. The BSM promotes two types of socialization: activities carried out by volunteers, association employees, and practitioners, and initiatives organized for the public. The first network, that is, that formed by volunteers, association employees, and practitioners, constitutes the core of the BSM, the muscle that drives the *bertsolaritza* phenomenon onward. The network encompasses verse schools, national and provincial *bertsolaritza* associations, and local supporters and organizers. These groups basically organize, support, and participate in *bertsolaritza* activities, but doing this requires a socialization network, first because networks provide necessary support for *bertsolaritza* activities, and second, because constructing and maintaining such networks is one of the BSM's main objectives. The movement therefore has two principal aims: to promote the art of *bertsolaritza* and to create social networks. They are like the movement's muscle and skeleton, mutually reinforcing each other to create the critical mass that strengthens the core of the BSM that, invigorated by that synergy, generates a ripple effect in its immediate environment.

Verse schools are a clear example of this. They are organized spaces for learning, and as such are located outside the former *natural* learning model. Furthermore, their work goes beyond mere transmission, since they integrate both participation and transmission into the same process. Miren Artetxe (2014) uses Lave and Wenger's (1991) community of practice to analyze verse schools, arriving at the conclusion that these institutions have the capacity to create friendship groups around *bertsolaritza* activities. Ainhoa Agirreazaldegi and Arkaitz Goikoetxea (2007) argue that verse schools not only transmit knowledge but also promote collaboration and leisure-time friendship groups.

Bertsolaritza schools do train future practitioners, and in that sense are key, but they also help generate and strengthen *bertsolaritza*'s critical mass, which is why so much emphasis is placed on creating friendship networks.

The Associations of Friends of *Bertsolaritza* (there is one national and five provincial associations) are vital components of the BSM. At the beginning, the first association (the national one) was mainly based on voluntary work, although there were a few employees. As associations have taken on more projects, their staff has grown (there are now more than seventy paid employees), but voluntary work remains essential in terms of coping with the workload and ensuring decision-making capacity, influence, and social expansion. The institutionalization that has resulted from the associations' success has increased both their size and the amount of financial support they receive from the public institutions, but this is a double-edged sword, at once enabling the establishment of better facilities and generating new problems and difficulties. The BSM claims that, on the one hand, by combining the efforts of both employees and volunteers they have been able to launch more projects more efficiently; yet on the other, the new situation has created coordination problems between the two groups, as well as posing a new challenge regarding the integration of the new generation into the institutionalized system of the associations, a system that is sometimes perceived not as a work in progress, but rather as a ready-built project in which there is little room for young people and their concerns.

Informational Strategy

The BSM does not subscribe to the usual public mobilization model. There are no standard protest gatherings. Since the BSM is first and foremost an art-based movement, it is *bertsolaritza*'s principal form of expression, namely the *bertso saioa*, which embodies what mobilization represents for other social movements. In fact, as stated earlier, *bertso saioas*, *bertsolaritza* events in which *bertsolaris* sing improvised rhymed verses in accordance with certain metrics in front of an audience, is the BSM's *action exemplaire*.

In order to promote mobilization, the BSM developed a two-pronged information strategy: the organization of *bertsolaritza* events and its media policy.

The importance of championships is paramount. They are the most popular *bertsolaritza* events in terms of both audience numbers and media impact. In fact, the Association of Friends of *Bertsolaritza* was initially created in the context of a debate about the main championship. Over recent decades, championships have been used as expansion tools in an increasingly informational way: all the BSM's core resources are mobilized to organize these events, which are intended to promote large-scale mobilization. Media policy is also used to help encourage mobilization. The BSM decides what media outlets to approach and how to do so. However, the strategy employed is not always geared toward expansion, and sometimes priority is given to other needs or issues. Lately, for instance, the BSM has engaged in a process of reflection and debate on the current championship model, which may be modified in the future even though these potential changes may result in a drop in audience numbers.

Examples of media policy reflect this expansion-contraction strategy more clearly. During its early years, the BSM focused on television, the dominant media at that time, and a very popular program was broadcast on the Basque public television about the art form. *Bertsolaritza* was already present on the radio and in the written press, but television was the key to increasing audience levels. A public mobilization with extensive media coverage was vital to reaching the living rooms of those who never attended *bertsolaritza* events, in order to encourage them, through the media also, to become audiences in squares, theaters, youth-managed buildings, auditoriums, or any other venue in which face-to-face sessions were held.

However, the aim was not only to appear in the media. Being an art-based phenomenon, the BSM required appropriate conditions to show its art form to its best advantage. The movement negotiated with the media to reach an agreement on the coverage that would be provided. This leverage was the direct result of the media policy enacted by the BSM: it was a collective initiative that was legitimized to negotiate and had solid criteria. In the 1990s, however, the Basque public television had a different set of criteria (for example, it wanted the right to broadcast the same *bertsolaritza* event as many times as it wanted), and since no agreement was reached, the events were not broadcast on television for almost two years. This hampered the expansion process and was the source of serious economic difficulties for the national Association of Friends of *Bertsolaritza*, because television rights constituted an important source of income. The association was forced to fire the only two employees it had at the time. The decision prioritized other needs, over and above expansion, with the Association of Friends of *Bertsolaritza* deciding to sacrifice short-term expansion in order to maintain appropriate conditions for its art form. It was a strategic decision that the association believed would reinforce the BSM's identity, enabling it to expand more effectively in the future. In fact, the decision proved beneficial for both the art and the social movement, giving rise to a greater degree of social recognition and prestige. When the *bertso-laritza* events were once again broadcast on public television, it was from a much stronger position than before.

There is much data to suggest that the BSM's information strategy was successful. As I have already shown, the number of events, practitioners, and followers increased, but in order to understand how this happened, it is interesting to analyze when the followers became followers and how they learned about *bertsolaritza*, since this will provide some insight into the consequences of the informational strategy.

According to a study conducted by Siadeco in 1993, almost half of *bertsolaritza* devotees did not become so at home, during their childhood years, but rather came to appreciate the art either at school or when they were adults. The results reported by Xabier Aierdi et al. (2007) are similar, finding that most followers became fond of *bertsolaritza* outside the scope of primary socialization, which occurs during childhood in the family context. The fact that they discovered the art form outside the family environment and/or when they were adults suggests that, in a period in which the former *natural* transmission spaces no longer exist, there must inevitably be some other dynamics at work in promoting the revitalization of the art. When the sources of information about *bertsolaritza* are analyzed, the importance of the media is striking: two out of three people (65 percent) claimed to receive information about *bertsolaritza* through the media, whereas only one out of three (33 percent) said they obtained said information from friends (Aierdi et al. 2007).

We can therefore conclude that the BSM's informational strategy was a determining factor in the revitalization of the art. However, the media age has changed drastically over recent years, and the decline of the television-based media model has forced the BSM to establish a new strategy offering new initiatory pathways, such as the *bertsoa.eus* model.

That Question by Touraine

Alain Touraine's (1985, 2004) concern is whether or not the collective actor emerges when a new problematic situation appears and certain agents start moving, and whether this collective actor is capable of becoming an autonomous subject that transforms its own situation. In the case of *bertsolaritza*, the answer to both questions seems to be yes. Because it belonged to an ecosystem that no longer existed, it was pushed toward extinction. A different cultural model prevailed and improvised verse singing was not widespread in hardly any of the new cultural contexts. However, it somehow managed to turn itself into a social movement based on an art form, operating exclusively and autonomously in the cultural field. This social movement has created spaces for transmission and participation, has encouraged the emergence of new practitioners, and has attracted more followers, as well as greater numbers of association employees and volunteers. It has mobilized masses, not for protest but rather for artistic-social events, has used the media to expand its influence and reach the living rooms of those who were not following the art in face-to-face sessions, and has created and socialized new ways of understanding the art based on a combination of social and artistic perspectives. As a result, the number of events, practitioners, and followers has grown, and the diversification process is becoming increasingly evident in terms of artistic production, types of events and the nature of the audience.

The BSM now faces a new set of problems, because all moments have their challenges. The following issues are particularly worth highlighting: (1) the BSM needs to find a way of responding to the increasingly heterogeneous tastes of *bertsolaritza* followers; (2) it must create the conditions required to enable younger generations to join the project and adapt it to their specific circumstances; (3) it must establish new transmission and promotion policies for the new multipolar media era; and (4) it must strive to incorporate innovative and peripheral gender-equality initiatives into the hegemonic discourse and practice of both the social movement itself and the artistic discipline.

Methods

The study was based on both qualitative and quantitative techniques: 2,867 questionnaires, 32 in-depth interviews, 3 focus groups, and one Delphi with

27 participants. It was conducted in two phases. Between 2005 and 2007, a total of 1,200 questionnaires were administered to Basque speakers, 723 questionnaires were administered to the audience at the Championship, and 344 questionnaires were completed by members of the public attending *bertsolaritza* events all year round. During the same period, one Delphi was conducted with 27 experts on *bertsolaritza* and 3 focus groups were held. Between 2015 and 2017, a further 600 questionnaires were completed by members of the audience at *bertsolaritza* events all year round, 32 in-depth interviews were held with *bertsolaritza* experts and we analyzed the quantitative data that has been collected by the Xenpelar Documentation Center since the 1980s.

Bibliography

Agirreazaldegi, Ainhoa, and Arkaitz Goikoetxea. 2007. "Verse Schools." *Oral Tradition* 22, no. 2: 65–68.

Aierdi, Xabier, Juan Aldaz, Eider Alkorta, Alfredo Retortillo, and Harkaitz Zubiri. 2007. *Bertsolaritza. Tradizio modernoa.* Bilbao: University of the Basque Country.

Armstrong, Elizabeth A., and Mary Bernstein. 2008. "Culture, Power, and Institutions: A Multi-Institutional Politics Approach to Social Movements." *Sociological Theory* 26, no. 1: 74–99.

Artetxe, Miren. 2014. "Bertsolaritzaren eragina Lapurdiko bertso-eskoletako gazteen identitatean eta hizkuntza erabileran: bertso-eskola Jarduera Komunitate gisa aztertzeko proposamena." *Bat:*

Soziolinguistika aldizkaria 92–93, nos. 3–4: 11–31.

Castells, Manuel. 1997. *The Power of Identity*. Oxford, UK: Blackwell.

———. 2015. Second Edition. *Networks of Outrage and Hope: Social Movements in the Internet Age*. Cambridge, UK; Malden, MA: Polity Press.

Foley, John M. 2007. "Basque Oral Poetry Championship." *Oral Tradition* 22, no. 2: 3–11.

Gamson, William A. 1975. *The Strategy of Social Protest*. Homewood, IL: Dorsey.

Garner, Roberta, and Mayer N. Zald. 2012. "Now We Are Almost Fifty! Reflections on a Theory of the Transformation of Social Movement Organizations." *Social Forces* 91, no. 1: 3–11.

Garzia, Joxerra. 2000. *Gaur egungo bertsolarien bali-abide poetiko-erretorikoak. Marko teorikoa eta aplikazio didaktikoa*. Bilbao: University of the Basque Country.

———. 2007. "Basque Oral Ecology." Oral Tradition 22, no. 2: 47–64.

———. 2012. *Bertsolaritza. El bertsolarismo. Bertsolaritza*. Donostia-San Sebastián: Etxepare Basque Institute.

Garzia, Joxerra, Jon Sarasua, and Andoni Egaña. 2001a. *Bat-bateko bertsolaritza. Gakoak eta azter-bideak*. Donostia: Bertsolari liburuak.

Garzia, Joxerra, Jon Sarasua, and Andoni Egaña. 2001b. *The Art of Bertsolaritza: Improvised Basque Verse Singing*. Donostia: Bertsolari liburuak.

Heidemann, Kai. 2012. "The View From Below: Exploring the Interface of Europeanization and Basque Language Activism in France." *Mobilization* 17, no. 2: 195–220.

———. 2014. "In the Name of Language: School-Based Language Revitalization, Strategic Solidarities, and State Power in the French Basque Country." *Journal of Language, Identity & Education* 13, no. 1: 53–69.

Hourigan, Niamh. 2001. "New Social Movement Theory and Minority Language Television Campaigns." *European Journal of Communication* 16, no. 1: 77–100.

Laclau, Ernesto. 2005. *On Populist Reason*. London: Verso.

Laclau, Ernesto, and Chantal Mouffe. 1985. *Phegemony and Socialist Strategy: Towards a Radical Democratic Politics*. London: Verso.

Lave, Jean, and Etienne Wenger. 1991. *Situated Learning: Legitimate Peripheral Participation*. Cambridge: Cambridge University Press.

MacAdam. 1982.

McCarthy, John D., and Mayer N. Zald. 1977. "Resource Mobilization and Social Movements: A Partial Theory." *American Journal of Sociology* 82, no. 6: 1212–41.

Melucci, Alberto. 1985. "The Symbolic Challenge of Contemporary Movements." *Social Research* 52, no. 4: 789–816.

———. 1989. *Nomads of the Present: Social Movements and Individual Needs in Contemporary Society*. London: Hutchinson Radius.

———. 1996. *Challenging Codes: Collective Action in the Information Age*. Cambridge, UK: Cambridge

University Press.

Mouffe, Chantal. 1984. "Towards a Theoretical Interpretation of New Social Movements." In *Rethinking Marx*, edited by Sakari Hänninen and Leena Paldán. New York: International General IMMRC.

Offe, Claus. 1985. "New Social Movements: Challenging the Boundaries of Institutional Politics." *Social Research* 52, no. 4: 817–68.

Polletta, Francesca, and James M. Jasper. "Collective Identity and Social Movements." *Annual Review of Sociology* 27: 283–305.

Rao, Hayagreeva, Calvin Morrill, and Mayer N. Zald. 2000. "Power Plays: How Social Movements and Collective Action Create New Organizational Forms." *Research in Organizational Behaviour* 22: 237–81.

Sarasua, Jon. 2004. "Bertsolaritzaren gizarte eta kultur ezaugarriak." *Ahozko inprobisazioa munduan topaketak 2003*. Donostia: Euskal Herriko Bertsozale Elkartea.

———. 2007. "Social Features of Bertsolaritza." *Oral Tradition* 22, no. 2: 33–46.

———. 2013. *Hiztunpolisa. Euskaltasunaren norabideaz apunteak*. Pamplona: Pamiela.

Siadeco. 1995. "Bertsozaletasunari buruzko azterketa." *Jakin* 87: 11–74.

Tilly, Charles. 1978. *From Mobilization to Revolution*. Reading, MA: Addison-Wesley.

Touraine, Alain. 1981. *The Voice and the Eye: An Analysis of Social Movements*. Cambridge, UK: Cambridge University Press.

————. 1985. "An Introduction to the Study of Social Movements." *Social Research* 52, no. 4: 749–87.

————. 2004. "On the Frontiers of Social Movements." *Current Sociology* 52, no. 4: 717–25.

Turner, Ralph H., and Lewis M. Killian. 1987. *Collective Behavior*. Englewood Cliffs, NJ: Prentice Hall.

Xenpelar Dokumentazio Zentroa. 2016.

Zald, Mayer. N., and Roberta Ash. 1966. "Social Movement Organizations: Growth, Decay and Change." *Social Forces* 44, no. 3: 327–41.

Zubiri, Harkaitz. 2010. "Euskara eta kultura-kont-sumoa." *Kultura 08-09*. Vitoria-Gasteiz: Eusko Jaurlaritzaren Argitalpen Zerbitzu Nagusia.

————. 2014. "The Consequences of Diglossia in the Cultural Habits of a Minority Language: Analysing the Consumption of Basque Culture." *Global Studies Journal* 6, no. 1: 67–77.

8

Be There, Take the Floor, Say Something: Bertsolaritza Schools, Agency, and Language Use

Miren Artetxe Sarasola

Let us imagine a bilingual society. Let us imagine that one of those two languages is a minoritized language. This is a description that fits the situation in the Basque Country, both in the Northern Basque Country (NBC) in France and in the Southern Basque Country in Spain. Let us continue imagining. Let us say that everybody in that society has language skills, to a greater or lesser degree, in the two languages mentioned. Although that situation is better than our current one, there, too, the key to minoritized language survival is its speakers' attitude and conduct: a certain number of speakers have to tend to use the minoritized language in order for it to survive. And the tendency to use that language—whether conscious or unconscious—is the result of daily choices. If Basque is to survive, then, there

* This is part of the dissertation I am working on, with a grant from Mintzola Fundazioa and Mikel Laboa Katedra. Support has also been provided by The Basque Government's Education, Language Policy, and Culture Department (IT-881-16).

is a need for speakers who tend to use it, and not just people who can get by in it. It is a fact, however, that current data about the use of Basque is worrying (Eusko Jaurlaritza 2013), and the transition from knowing the language to actually using it has not been as automatic as had been expected. From the Basque sociolinguistic perspective, motivation, knowledge, and use have been seen as the key elements (Sánchez Carrión 1987). However, until the present those factors have seldom been examined in an integrated way: "The links between them have been sensed, and their existence declared, but how are they actually connected in practice? How does the leap from one to the other take place? Or, on the contrary, what type of gaps are there between those dimensions, gaps that affect them mutually?" (Hernández 2016, 188)

In this chapter I will try to explain several ideas I have developed during the research I am currently carrying out that may lead us toward the answers to those questions. In fact, the objective of my research is to examine how the tendency to use Basque is constructed and how it is maintained, particularly among young *bertsolaris* or oral improvisers in the NBC. The current-day language landscape in the NBC is not promising but, although there is a low density of Basque-speakers, there are several oases for Basque. One of them is the Seaska school network, another the *bertsolaritza*—or oral improvisation—school network and the bertsolaritza movement in general that, although smaller, may be more tightly woven. Young Bertsolaritza school (BS) pupils (from the ages of seventeen to twenty), all of them Seaska pupils and former pupils, are the subjects of this research.[1] In fact, the research question is based on an observation: In addition to having a firm discourse in favor of the revival of Basque, young people at BS also have a proactive attitude to the use of Basque: they have decided to live in Basque, and, in order to do so, they take their everyday language decisions in an active manner. In my work, then, I will try to identify some of the major factors that may be behind these young people's proactive attitude toward Basque.[2]

Therefore, as I said, in what follows I will outline the key ideas of my work up to now. To do so, first, I will try to explain several concepts related to

---

1. This chapter is based on fifteen interviews and three years of fieldwork. The informers come from different linguistic origins (Basque is not the only home language for all of them), but they have all gone to language immersion schools. Some of them have been improvising since they were small children, while others started recently, and all of them have been participants in the bertsolaritza school at the Bernat Etxepare High School in Baiona.

2. Although the term "proactive" is mostly used in the work and institutional area, it is increasingly used in sociolinguistic psycholinguistics as well. The concept addresses individuals' active control of their attitude, in contrast to a reactive attitude to taking decisions, an attitude that depends on context and structure. I have not used the term in an absolute sense: no decisions are taken without any reference to the context. What I want to state with this term is that although the options that the context offers may not be diverse, they do seek out even the slightest opportunities, and in an active manner, in order to make choices that favor Basque.

language use, concepts that I believe will be needed in later analysis; second, I will explain how bertso activities influence BS pupils with regard to language attitudes and behavior, analyzing BSs as communities of practice.

Language Behavior, Motivation, Experienced Identity, and Agency

The factors that influence bilingual speakers to choose one language or another at a particular moment have been examined from various different points of view (perhaps mostly from a psycholinguistics perspective), and in our context work has been carried out to classify and model the factors that influence language use from a sociolinguistic point of view.[3] Three areas are usually taken into account: social structure (with regard to the language's place and image in society, in other words, demographic, economic, political, legal, and cultural factors, among others); relationship networks and interaction areas (where, with whom, the subject under discussion, and so on); and the speaker or individual. From Anthony Giddens' duality of structure perspective, when a language becomes a paradigm for socialization, on the other hand, there is little point in making distinctions: individuals' characteristics are developed in their immediate surroundings, and those surroundings are developed within a larger structure and, at the same

---

3. I will refer to two pieces of research on the Basque Country in my analysis below: Jean Baptiste Coyos' theoretical model (Coyos 2007) and Iñaki Martínez de Luna's proposed model (Martínez de Luna 2004).

time, each individual's characteristics can affect those surroundings and that structure (Giddens 1979).

It cannot be denied that when decisions are taken, there are social conditions in addition to each individual's ability to choose: "they will use one language or another depending, on the one hand, on their priorities, wishes, values, and needs; on the other, the material and nonmaterial costs involved in each choice also condition each decision" (Grin 1990, 155, in Erize 2016, 118–19).

This language-choice dilemma has been examined in Basque sociolinguistics in terms of attitude to language use and motivation. And, with regard to motivation, in particular, two types of motivation have been differentiated: integrative and instrumental motivation. An integrative attitude is linked to symbolic motivation, and it has also been defined as being *identity creating* in our context (Martínez de Luna 2004). This type of motivation is usually defined in terms of attachment with regard to language, communication between speakers, certain groups, and cultural and social customs. Instrumental motivation, on the other hand, is connected to "the possibility of increasing social scale opportunities and economic advantages" as a result of using a particular language variety (Joly and Uranga 2010).

The main motivation, then, to use a minority language is integrative (leaving the language competence factor to one side), bearing in mind that the instrumental motivation has very little influence in our case (Martínez de Luna 2004). In the general context of the NBC, it is very clear that knowing and using Basque brings very few social advantages, whereas there are many great advantages to using French. That being the case, it is obvious that without integrative motivation it will be very difficult to promote a tendency to speak in Basque.

As Iñaki Martínez de Luna himself points out, however, integrative motivation by itself is not strong enough, and "has to be put through the sieve of reality" (Martínez de Luna 2001). This is in fact the main problem: "although *identity creating* motivations are among the strongest, by themselves they are not enough to turn reality around" (Martínez de Luna 2004).

In this area, I think that the question that Jone Miren Hernández raises in order to understand the gap between knowledge and use is relevant: "what is the basis for one attitude or another at its starting point? What does it take to *motivate me*? What keeps my interest and commitment to Basque? (Hernández 2016a, 182). This is the key that Xabier Erize suggests: "In any case, bearing in mind that motivation is something internal, motivating from the outside is difficult and, in order for it to be successful, that external motivation must connect with something inside the person; otherwise, it is very difficult to achieve anything" (Erize 2016, 121).

The differentiation between identity creating and instrumental motivation or between internal and external motivations is concurrent with a concept of agency brought from psychological anthropology to social sciences.[4] I find Sherry Ortner's interpretation of this concept particularly interesting. Ortner believes that subjectivity is the essence of agency; in other words, agency is not a desire in itself but, rather, desires and intentions within the framework of feelings and thoughts, which are both constructed socially. This author understands agency as an "effect of critical subjectivity in action" to the extent to which the subject sees difficulties in his/her context (Ortner 2006).

From an anthropological perspective, several authors believe that the basis to general identification is the *experienced identity* (Terradas 2009). Thus language and national identity, for instance, are derived from real-life experience identity:

What is experienced identity? It is human recognition of life that is mainly based on memory of experiences had, their repercussions on feelings, and the feelings of belonging and connection that that memory requires. Experienced identity is the basis for cultural identity, which is never either wholly individual or wholly collective. It emerges halfway along the road between the memory of personal meanings and shared chronotope memories (Terradas 2009, 63–64).

The sentimental attachments, emotions and affection that emerge from things we do in daily life

---

4. Anthony Giddens and Pierre Bourdieu, for example, have used the same concept to research agents' influence on the production and reproduction of social systems (Duranti 2004, 452).

make our *experienced identity*, and on that foundation we build our other identities such as language,
culture, and national identities (which give rise to
identity creating motivation). Identity is not something that we are given beforehand; it is, rather,
something that results from things we do and do
again (Butler 1990). The *performative turn* has led us
to understand identity as something that is continually defined and redefined. From that perspective,
then, language identity must also be understood in a
dynamic way: depending on the language we use, we
develop one language identity or another, and this
will change if we change our language habits. We develop *identity creating* motivation through our (language) habits in the micro-spaces in our everyday
environment or community of practice.

Individuals participate in multiple communities
of practice, and individual identity is based on the
multiplicity of this participation. Rather than seeing
the individual as some disconnected entity floating
around in social space, or as a location in a network,
or as a member of a particular group or set of groups,
or as a bundle of social characteristics, we need to
focus on communities of practice. Such a focus allows us to see the individual as an actor articulating
a range of forms of participation in multiple communities of practice (Eckert and McConnell-Ginet
1992, 8).

However, from the sociolinguistic perspective
we often forget that the speaker, the individual, is a
body, and everything we have lived through has been
as a body, and from a body. As Mari Luz Esteban

underlines, recent theories and methodologies have made the body a central issue. From that point of view, the body is seen as an agent, in other words, as "a bridge between structure and practice" (Esteban 2010). When the scientific paradigm—which sees the mind and the body as well as rationality and emotionality in a dichotomous way—moves the body to the center of the paradigm, emotions, too, become objects of research. In fact, the body and the emotions are taken as the basis for inter-subjectivity, and thus, for identity construction (Esteban 2011, 29).

Before moving from these conceptual considerations to reflections about my research, let me say that I have chosen to analyze BSs as communities of practice, with the objective of examining the language identity construction process in a group that is created and structured around the practice or bertsolaritza.[5] A decade after Jean Lave and Etienne Wenger (1991) created the concept of community of practice, Penelope Eckert and Sally McConnell-Ginet revisit it in their research about language and identity construction (Eckert 2001; Eckert and McConnell-Ginet 1992; Eckert and McConnell-Ginet 1995), defining it as: "An aggregate of people who come together around mutual engagement in an endeavour. Ways of doing things, ways of talking, beliefs, values, power relations in short practices emerge in the course of this mutual endeavor" (Eckert and McConnell-Ginet 1992, 464). In our case, thanks to this concept as defended by Hernández (2007) and

---

5. For more information about the choice of analyzing BSs as communities of practice, see Artetxe (2014).

Paula Kasares (2013), identity has been analyzed as an element constructed by practice.

From this position, and with the intention of analyzing the language behavior phenomenon in a more complex way, I will explain several phenomena that take place in BSs: for one thing, I will bring up the fact that there is a link between the feeling of agency and the presence of the body, the voice and the fact that we create a discourse while we sing improvised verses. For another, I will put forward the notion that individual and collective experiences of agency can influence language behavior.

Bertsolaritza School: Being There, Taking the Floor

Let us begin at the beginning. Subjectivity and identity are embodied through practice. So far so good. But which practices are carried out at BSs? Around which practices is the community constructed?[6]

Firstly, a group comes together at the BS. Individuals decide whether to go there in their free time: it is a leisure activity. Some of them have been going to the BS for years. Others have just begun. The BS can be described as a place for developing bertsolaritza skills, but it could not be adequately defined without specifying that it is also a space for pleasure.

---

6. In this chapter, rather than analyzing what is done at the BS, I will make use of an actual BS session in order to offer meaningful examples, based on an observation carried out at Bernat Etxepare High School on March 5, 2014.

There was already a good atmosphere among us all, a really good atmosphere during our three years at high school, and at the beginning we used to go to the bertsolaritza school with the intention of thinking up verses, but. . . I don't know how many hours we've spent there, laughing out loud, talking about I don't know what, discussing things, having our afternoon snack. . . So we did use to go to the bertsolaritza school, but it's not just limited to that, there are hundreds of other things you can do as well as verses.

—*Boy [I], seventeen years old. Member of the bertsolaritza school at Bernat Etxepare High School (Baiona).*

Members of the BS meet up at the school gates and get chatting there. The teacher comes and the atmosphere doesn't change: we say hello in a friendly way, and we all head to the classroom, talking all the way. When we're in there, we move the tables and chairs around and put the chairs into a circle. And then "So, shall we start?" is what you hear, and the teacher gives us an exercise: someone will stand up and say a word, which will be the base for the rhyme, and somebody else starts a verse off. As soon as this other improviser sings some words, the next member gives the next rhymed word and so on, until the stanza is completed. The first one completes the stanza and starts the humor off: some by choosing the rhymed word (by mentioning events external to the school, and making the others sing about that), others by singing the verses that make up the rhyme (making an effort to get over the obstacles set up). Laughter is heard from verse to verse and after hearing the rhymes set for each improviser. You hear comments about the verses. And applause when the verses are good. Some rhymes lead to discussions. "Lakona," "Lakabe," Zutabe."[7]

Bertsolaritza as a social practice involves features that make it easy to enjoy it and feel emotions: the disassociation between composing and performing, the disassociation between the creator and the audience, and the disassociation between the individual and the community becomes fuzzy (Casals 2009), and mutual connections and feelings of identification are strengthened: "oral improvisation, as a playful activity that consists of an unavoidable functionality, has been seen to be a generator of group identities and modifications in individual identities" (Casals 2010, 6).

Defining them as places and times for pleasure gives us the basis for examining the activities that are carried out there: the subjects build a positive narrative about what takes place there. In other words, starting with the emotional repercussions that the subjects feel there (Terrades 2004) and identification with the group, the BS is a suitable place for building individual identity (Artetxe 2014).

"Who wants to sing now?" says the teacher. After some warm-up exercises, it is time to begin in a more

---

7. "Lakona" is a breed of sheep; "Lakabe" is an occupied town; the word "zutabe" means column, but is also the title of ETA's printed bulletin (*Zutabe*).

serious way. Now two people are going to sing about a topic, and the others will listen. "Alright, L and A stand up, ok?" They both get up, prop themselves on the table in front of the others, who are in a circle. "You're a fifteen-year old girl, A, and it's the first time you're going out at night. Luckily, L, your sister, who's eighteen and used to going out, has come out with you." They agree who is to begin. The teacher tells them to stand up, and suggests they take the microphone (a broom resting against a chair). Some people think that's a good idea, but A and L prefer not to use it.

Improvising verses involves moving out of the group and standing somewhere the others can see them. After hearing the subject, they think about what they are going to say, and start to sing. Improvising verses thus leads to becoming the center of attention in public. Your presence itself is under examination: your body, your position, movements, and gestures. And knowing how to be there is another necessary skill in *bertsolaritza*. An example of that can be seen at the BS where, although there is no explicit training in managing emotions, the *bertsolaris* are asked to know how to feel comfortable under the others' gaze: "As well as the ability and skill to improvise verses, beginners are taught how to adopt typical bertsolari postures and use typical techniques" (Esteban 2004, 198). So the body, even if in negative terms, is the improvisational improviser's first tool (Alberdi 2012), and putting their body in front of others influences themselves and the others.

Alessandro Duranti states that presence is a type of individual agency that affects everybody: "human presence is something that must be reckoned with by others and therefore implies the power to affect others" (Duranti 2004, 455). In fact, this author confirms different levels of agency during performances. And the first level, in fact, is the individual's self-affirmation or "ego-affirming" level. Duranti mentions two things on this level: presence and voice: "A and B agree on a melody and concentrate, looking down at the floor. The other people, carry on chatting for a while in a respectful but—at the same time—informal tone of voice. Then they realise that A is ready to start the verse from the look on her face. They keep quiet and look at her. Another twenty seconds go by, and then A starts singing." Her voice, in both speech and song, is a coordinated action of her whole body. The voice and respiratory system, the digestive system, vocal resonators, and many muscle groups are used to project the voice. Creating a voice is not one of this area's main function. The voice, however, is the immediate expression of our identity: "an irreducible sign of identity" (Merleau-Ponty 1970).

And, as well as being a sign of identity, bringing your voice out is also an action of self-affirmation for the individual. Speaking in itself denotes agency:

> The very act of speaking in front of others who can perceive such an act establishes the speaker as a being whose existence must be reckoned with in terms of his or her communicative goals and abilities. As the most sophisticated form of human expression,

language use implies that its users are entities that must also possess other human qualities including the ability to affect their own and others' ways of being. Hence, this most basic level of agency—an agency of an existential sort which, however, needs others (whether as a real or imaginary audience)—does not need to rely on referential or denotational meaning. It is language per se as a human faculty rather than the meaning of its words that is sufficient for agency as ego-affirming to be at work. (Duranti 2004, 455)

Inevitably, then, taking turn to speak is an affirmation of the individual's character: *This is me, I'm here and this is my voice.* And this "both affirms the speaker qua speaker and reveals human qualities" (Duranti 2004, 459). Thus the experience of speaking is not neutral , and learning to have confidence in oneself is also learning to improvise:

> The bertsolaritza school has given me this . . . The way I am . . . *M.A.S.: What?* I don't know . . . It's a lot of things. Perhaps I know myself better now . . . I've gotten rid of that timidity, or I'm trying to, trying to have more self-confidence.
> —*Girl [P], seventeen years old. Member of the bertsolaritza school at Bernat Etxepare High School (Baiona).*

And if we look beyond speaking in public, to singing verses (or, as Marta Font defines it, poetic *performance*), agency takes on another dimension

that can become a subversive experience, both in-
wards and outwards (Font 2011).

After L's first verse, A spends a long time thinking.
People look at him, and he says "-ela." The suggestions come straightaway: "gela," "arbela," "horrela,"
"epela," "itzela," "txapela" . . . They are still shouting
out rhymes as A starts singing. Another two verses,
and the two-bertsolari session has finished. The
members who are listening sing out the repetition of
the last line at greater volume than before, giving the
session a happy ending. The applause, too, is louder
than before.

Learning to improvise is learning the technique
in order to improvise verses. But making verses involves more than that, as the objective of improvising
is actually saying something pertinent. The bertsolari needs to master technique in order to be able to
create a discourse. Jon Sarasua, Andoni Egaña, and
Joserra Gartzia, who have carried out considerable
work developing and transmitting the theoretical
bertsolaritza corpus, place bertsolaritza's rhetorical
and poetic value above its technical value (Gartzia,
Sarasua, and Egaña 2001).

> With regard to content, the need to cre-
> ate discourse clearly calls for reflection: the
> bertsolaris have to deal with a subject, place
> themselves in a situation, or give an opinion.
> Bertsolaris have to choose what to say and
> how to say it, and then try to be true to that
> decision, respecting the verses' formal lim-
> itations. The dynamic of reflection created
> during the poetic dialogue process is even

more interesting. During an artificially created dialogue situation, what Eric Dicharry
calls "twofold intellectual decentralization"
takes place (Dicharry 2013, 65). On one hand,
the poet has to distance him/herself from his/
her own point of view, forced to interpret or
play a certain personality or situation, and on
the other, he/she has to place him/herself in
relation to the fellow bertsolari's point of view.

That makes you think, ideas and so on,
"What would I say there?" and then you have
to think it through. And, well, we think it
through . . . And when we listen to the others,
too. "Oh, yeah!"

*Boy [K], fifteen years old. Member of the
bertsolaritza school at Bernat EtxepareHigh
School (Baiona).*

Half an hour has already passed since they came
chatting into the room. They've all sung one by one
during the first exercise, then a first round in pairs,
and it's time to do the second round. First they had to
sing in the *zortziko handi* meter (four rhymes, long
verses), and now it's a *zortziko txiki* (four rhymes,
short verses). It's advisable for different meters. A
and J have gotten up, stood in front of the others,
and the teacher has given them their subject: "You've
been classmates since you were little. You can't stand
each other. You've started at high school this year,
and today's your first day at class. The teacher tells
you where to sit when you come in . . . And you're
next to each other." A thinks of an idea straightaway.

You can see that in her facial expression. "J starts," says the teacher. "A has an idea," answers J. He does not have any ideas, and wants A to begin. "Ok, A can start!" says the teacher.

A specific idea come from a single word, an image, a memory, or a sensation. And if you think it is a good idea, that is because you confer an expressive force to that idea. A potential expressivity. However, you have to say it using a specific number of syllables. Using specific words. In a specific order. So there is a specific aesthetic.

After thirty seconds, A begins: "Erakasle honetaz, ezin ginen fida/ Ta hala ikusi dut arbelan begira/ Hartu regla eskutan, mugitu kadira/ hasieratik limitak markatu behar dira"["We can't trust this teacher / I've seen that on the board / Pick up your ruler, move your chair / You have to draw the lines from the start"]. Laughter is heard. The people sitting down act the situation out. They look at each other aggressively, as if they wanted to be as far apart from each other as possible. More laughter. And silence once more. Now it is J's turn.

The second agency level that Duranti mentions is "Act-constituting agency." Duranti pays special attention, however, to the creative power of poetry, singing, theater, humor from daily life, and narrative: "This is a dimension where speakers/singers/actors/story-tellers exploit some taken for granted or hidden properties of language, transforming our ordinary understanding of language and its relation to reality" (Duranti 2004, 459). In these genres "language users [are] accountable for the form of their expressions and the style of delivery" (Duranti 2004, 459).

The person singing the verses, however, chooses a way to say what he/she wants to, taking on the role assigned, putting together the best possible idea and expressed in the best possible way, respecting the formal limits or, perhaps more accurately, making use of them. In fact, bertsolaritza's symbolic strength is based on those formal limits. Being able to say things within those limits gives the message its strength: "Poetically organized discourse (POD) and, in general, poetic procedures may be regarded as a special way of formalizing speech by means of a number of constraints on how the text is organized—such as meter, rhythm, morphosyntactic parallelism, assonance, and other procedures—. . . Such constraints, that often occur together, heighten and specialize the symbolic impact of an utterance" (Banti and Giannattasio 2004).

But J starts to get nervous right away. He can't think of anything. "I don't know what to say," he says. The others keep quiet. They don't want to say anything right away. It seems they would rather he tried and managed it by himself. But they have stopped their theatrics. Time passes slowly. A minute. Two minutes. "Come on, J!" says the teacher. "I really can't think of anything." When he gives up, the others start shouting ideas out. "You'll get on better as time goes by." "Really that's what you wanted, being side-by-side." Laughter once more. Everyone relaxes. Conversations start up once more while J gets his verse ready. "Gela hontan badira ikasleak hogeita hamar / ta nik zure ondoan nuen erori behar / ezin gira soporta bizi osoan zehar/hori jakin nuelaik in nuen negar!" ["There are thirty pupils in this room / And I have to sit next to you / We can't stand each other / I cried when I found out"]. There is applause and shouts of encouragement in the room. "That's it, that's it!" "Great stuff, J!" J breathes a great sigh of relief. He is not satisfied, and the others know that too. They all feel a little frustrated.

As we have seen, improvising a *bertso* puts the individual on show. First, your body in front of the group. When the singing starts, each person's voice, and the internal situation that each voice expresses. Ideas, and the ways chosen to express them. Furthermore, the bertsolari may make a mess of the formal aspects of the creative process. Getting stuck. Making obvious mistakes. Or not. Even if there are no problems, even if you have to sing about a subject you know about and from a role you are familiar with, each person has to choose an idea and, so, the others, the listeners, will decide whether the idea is appropriate and whether it has been well expressed, and the *bertsolari* knows that from the moment he/she stands up.

Therefore, from the moment he/she dares to make verses until after singing, he/she has the sensation of being evaluated (by him/herself and by the others), and that gives rise to emotions in the *bertsolari*'s body as well as in those of the listeners, through empathy. As Hernández underlines, bertsolaritza does take the improvisers' bodies and emotions—as well as those of the listeners—to be an essential part of the whole. Thus for agency performance, there is no alternative to taking the risk of making mistakes. Making decisions, and living with them. If there were no evaluation, there would be no agency. Duranti, in fact, puts forward the following characteristics for defining agency: "Agency is here understood as the property of those entities (i) that have some degree of control over their own behaviour, (ii) whose actions in the world affect other entities' (and sometimes their own), and (iii) whose actions are the object of evaluation (e.g. in terms of their responsibility for a given outcome)" (Duranti 2004, 453).

As the BS is something that is held every week, and its members are not forced to attend, it is reasonable to suppose that, in that context, it is an emotionally bearable experience for them, both when singing and when listening. Although experiences outside the BS may be very different, the young people interpret the BS as an opportunity for agency performance.

> I know the other members of our school very well, so I don't mind about singing badly or well, doing this or that. Knowing the others better removes that timidity about singing in front our your bertsolaritza school classmates . . . I'm the first person to put my foot in it, so I know only too well that when I do, they don't say "Oh! You did that badly;" they're more likely to say "You should have done it another way." But without mocking you, or anything like that.

> *—Boy [I], seventeen years old. Member of the bertsolaritza school at Bernat Etxepare High School (Baiona).*

I do get nervous at bertsolaritza school because I put myself under pressure, but then I know they aren't going to judge me, so I'm relaxed with the others. But nervous, too, because I demand things of myself, but I know the teacher won't say anything bad, the others won't say I've done it badly and they'll help me, we'll help each other.

> *—Girl [N], seventeen years old. Member of the bertsolaritza school at Bernat Etxepare High School (Baiona).*

Those young people are aware of the agency experience they get at the BS, and their discourse both reflects that and influences them:

Bertsolaritza has given me self-confidence, I've seen I can do it and I sometimes even reach the championship, and that gives you a positive image of yourself.

> *—Girl [N], seventeen years old. Member of the bertsolaritza school at Bernat Etxepare High School (Baiona).*

It is even more than that. Empathy based on inter-subjectivity determines the group identity of the BS community of practice, and, at the same time, identifying agency experience also leads to each person identifying him/herself as an agent. This is why the expression "I'm in the BS" was mentioned a lot in the interviews.

Well, thanks to the bertsolaritza school, I don't know, I think... Yeah, our bertsolaritza school, for instance, makes me feel good, and then... really when we are at the bertsolaritza school, or bertsolaritza summer camps, or anything connected with bertsolaritza, it's me, it's really me, well, I don't know how to put it.

—Girl [M], seventeen years old. Member of the bertsolaritza school at Bernat Etxepare High School (Baiona).

There is positive identity in that "It's really me." This "I" is an agent capable of performing in front of others, making choices, and seeing itself to be capable. And affinities and identifications are developed along with that experienced positive identity.

In the end, people are a bit like you. And... yeah. That's more than just acceptance, confidence, or something like that... It's not confidence, it's more than that. I mean it's really something amazing.

—Girl [U], seventeen years old. Member of the bertsolaritza school at Bernat Etxepare High School (Baiona).

Why do I actually have a good time? Well, because I like bertsolaritza, but, you know, the people... That's it, you trust each other, and they're like you, so you identify with them right away, and... you have an amazing relationship with the people.

—Girl [U], seventeen years old. Member of the bertsolaritza school at Bernat Etxepare High School (Baiona).

Conclusion: Experienced Agency and Language Behavior

Viviani has researched popular young musicians in La Plata, Argentina, and states that "the musical experience empowers young people, and take shape in different moments of everyday life, not only in those specifically linked with musical experience" (Viviani 2014, 210). In other words, this author believes that "this experience and the possibilities which it offers make up emotional structures and behaviour patterns which later affect other areas of the young people's lives" (Viviani 2014, 210–11).

> I believe that we have the ability to communicate within the group and to do things in group, and that's important . . . Bertsolaris do have the ability to communicate well, that's it. And then, well. . . I don't know, feeling involved or something . . . In general, in life the way other people look at you [worries me], really a lot, so I don't dare to do some things, and bertsolaritza really helps me to do more things.
> *—Girl [N], seventeen years old. Member of the bertsolaritza school at Bernat Etxepare High School (Baiona).*

Maybe, well, the way we sing in front of people, we find it easy to explain what we need and so on. So sometimes we do stand up to the [high school] teacher.
—Boy [K], fifteen years old. Member of the bertsolaritza school at Bernat Etxepare High School (Baiona).

It's true that at secondary school, for instance, there are different groups, Baxoa Euskaraz [the movement if favor of being able to take university access examinations in Basque], the radio, some other types of groups, and the bertsolaritza school gives life to absolutely all of those groups, no doubt about that, I don't know why.
—Boy [A], seventeen years old. Member of the bertsolaritza school at Bernat Etxepare High School (Baiona).

More research needs to be done on how or to what extent that individual and collective agency experience shows itself outside the BS, outside in general. But it can be affirmed that it does influence language use.

The individual's agency, identification with others, and the group's and with individual's positive identities are all elements I have mentioned as factors that define the BS as a community of practice. But they are not the only factors because those experiences happening in Basque is no mere detail. Another meaningful feature of the BS community of practice is that communication among the members of the BS takes place in Basque. And, what is more, the pretext or reason for coming together uses Basque as an essential element of the activity itself. In any case, the experiences of group members related to those practices are also experiences lived out in Basque, and language experiences cannot be separated from other experiences. Thus the agency sensation, among other things, is something that the young people have experienced in Basque and that influences their attitude to the language:

> It was the only moment in the week when I felt myself . . . and it just happened to be the only moment of the week when I was doing something in Basque. . . . I felt myself, I felt accepted, I felt really good.
> —*Girl [N], seventeen years old. Member of the bertsolaritza school at Bernat Etxepare High School (Baiona).*

As mentioned at the beginning of the chapter, other types of identification, including language identity, are based on experienced identity. At the BS, these young bertsolaris experience agency, and experience it in Basque. Language identity is thus constructed in relation to this experience of agency, which enhances *identity creating* motivation. At the same time, the basis for a proactive language behavior with regard to language choice is individuals and groups acting as agents. My point is that experiencing agency in the BS can lead to seeing oneself as an agent in other aspects of social life.

If you go to a good bertsolaritza school, well, I don't know how to put it, I don't know what a good bertsolaritza school is, but, if there's a good atmosphere at the bertsolaritza school, you have to take that outside with you too, and you reflect that to other people, and . . . And I don't think it's enough for you to say to yourself "I'm going to speak in Basque;" well, I think, me for example, I know I'm not strong enough to say to myself "Hey, from now on I'm going to speak in Basque;" well, no, well, I need to feel my friends are there . . . I don't know if I'd be strong enough to do that by myself, well, I don't know what would happen if I wasn't at the bertsolaritza school.

Girl [L], seventeen years old. Member of the bertsolaritza school at Bernat Etxepare High School (Baiona).

Bibliography

Alberdi, Uxue. 2012. "Gorputzak, gorpuzkerak eta gorputzaldiak. Bertsolaritzan." In *Gorputza eta Generoa Euskal kulturan eta literaturan*, edited by Amaia Alvarez Uria and Gema Lasarte Leonet. Bilbao: UEU.

Artetxe, Miren. 2014. "Bertsolaritzaren eragina Lapurdiko bertso-eskoletako gazteen identitatean eta hizkuntza erabileran: bertso-eskola Jarduera Komunitate gisa aztertzeko proposamena." *Bat: Soziolinguistika Aldizkaria* 92–93, nos. 3–4: 11–31.

Banti, Giorgio, and Francesco Giannattasio. 2004. "Poetry." In *A Companion to Linguistic Anthropology*, edited by Alessandro Duranti. Oxford: Blackwell.

Boix-Fuster, Emili. 1993. *Triar no és trair: identitat i llengua en els joves de Barcelona*. Barcelona: Edicions 62.

Casals, Albert. 2009. "La cançó amb text improvisat: disseny i experimentació d'una proposta interdisciplinària per a Primària." PhD diss., Autonomous University of Barcelona.

———., coord. 2010. *Corrandescola: proposta didàctica per treballar la glosa a l'escola*. Cerdanyola del Vallès: ICE-UAB.

Coyos, Jean-Baptiste. 2007. "*Écart entre connaissance et usage d'une langue minoritaire: modèles théoriques et cas de la langue basque.* " In *Variable territoriale et promotion des langues minoritaires*, edited by Alain Viaut. Pessac: Maison des Sciences de l'Homme d'Aquitaine.

Dicharry, Eric. 2013.

Duranti, Alessandro. 2004. "Agency in Language." In *A Companion to Linguistic Anthropology*, edited by Alessandro Duranti. Oxford: Blackwell.

Eckert, Penelope. 2001. *Linguistic Variation as Social Practice: The Linguistic Construction of Identity in Belten High*. Malden, MA and Oxford: Blackwell.

Eckert, Penelope, and Sally McConnell-Ginet. 1992. "Think Practically and Look Locally: Language and Gender as Community-based Practice." *Annual Review of Anthropology* 21: 461–90.

————. 1995. "Constructing Meaning, Constructing Selves." *Gender Articulated: Language and the Socially Constructed Self*, edited by Kira Hall and Mary Bucholtz. New York and London: Routledge.

Erize, Xabier. 2016. "Euskal herritarren portaera linguistikoen motibo subjektiboen bilakaera (1991–2015), eta aurrera begirako bideak." *Bat: Soziolinguistika aldizkaria* 99: 113–77.

Esteban, Mari Luz. 2010. "Anthropology of the Body, Corporeal Itineraries, and Gender Relations." In *Feminist Challenges in the Social Sciences: Gender Studies in the Basque Country*, edited by Mari Luz Esteban and Mila Amurrio. Reno: Center for Basque Studies, University of Nevada, Reno; published in conjunction with the University of the Basque Country.

————. 2011. "Munduan adi egoteko modu bat. Euskal kulturaren jakintzen itsaso zabalean genero, gorputz eta emozioen ariketa antropologikoa." Unpublished ms.

Eusko Jaurlaritza. 2013. *Vè Enquête Sociolinguistique 2011*. Vitoria-Gasteiz: Eusko Jaurlaritzaren Argitalpen Zerbitzu Nagusia.

Font, Marta. 2011.

Frechina, Josep Vicent. 2014. *Pensar en vers. La cançó improvisada als països de la mediterrània*. Reus: Els Llibres de Caramella.

Gartzia, Joxerra, Jon Sarasua, and Andoni Egaña. 2001. *Bat bateko bertsolaritza. Gakoak eta azterbideak*. Andoain: Bertsolari liburuak.

Giddens, Anthony. 1979. *Central Problems in Social Theory: Action, Structure, and Contradiction in Social Analysis*. London and Basingstoke: The Macmillan Press.

Hernández García, Jone M. 2007. *Euskara, comunidad e identidad: elementos de transmisión, elementos de transgresión*. Madrid: Ministerio de Educación, Cultura y Deporte. Área de Cultura.

――――. 2016a. "Jarrera eta motibazio kontzeptuen haratago…: Hizkuntza kultura, praktikak eta emozioak." *Bat: Soziolinguistika aldizkaria* 99: 179–95.

――――. 2016b. "Odolak badu generorik? Edo zergatik gorputz emeak ez diren bertsoetarako bizitoki." In *Etnografia feministak Euskal Herrian. XXI. Mendera begira dagoen antropologia*, coordinated by Mari Luz Esteban and Jone M. Hernández. Bilbo: Udako Euskal Unibertsitatea eta Euskal Herriko Unibertsitatea.

Joly, Lionel, and Belen Uranga. 2010. "Hizkuntza-ideologia eta hizkuntza-jarrerak." In Arkaitz Zarraga et al., *Soziolinguistika eskuliburua*. Vitoria-Gasteiz: Soziolinguistika Klusterra.

Kasares, Paula. 2013. "Euskaldun hazi Nafarroan. Euskararen belaunez belauneko jarraipena eta hizkuntza sozializazioa familia euskaldunetan." PhD diss., Public University of Navarre.

Lave, Jean, and Etienne Wenger. 1991. *Situated Learning: Legitimate Peripheral Participation*. Cambridge: Cambridge University Press.

Martínez De Luna, Iñaki. 2001. "Euskal Herriko gaztetxoen hizkuntz egoera aztertzeko eredu orokorraren proposamena." *Bat: Soziolinguistika aldizkaria* 40: 47–66.

———. 2004. "Euskararen erabilera egokirako gizarte baldintzak." In *Egokitasuna hizkuntzaren erabileran. VIII. Jardunaldiak*, edited by Kaxildo Alkorta and Eneko Barrutia Etxebarria. Bilbao: Mendebalde Euskal Kultur Alkartea.

Merleau-Ponty, Maurice. 1970. *Lo visible y lo invisible*. Barcelona: Seix Barral.

Ortner, Sherry B. 2006. *Anthropology and Social Theory: Culture, Power, and the Acting Subject*. Durham: Duke University Press.

Sánchez Carrión, José María. 1987. *Un futuro para nuestro pasado. Claves para la recuperación del Euskara y teoría social de las Lenguas*. Lizarra: N.P..

Soziolinguistika Klusterra. 2011. *Gazteen hizkuntza erabileran kokatu eta bertan esku-hartzeko gida. Erabileraren GPSa*. N.P.: Soziolinguistika Klusterra.

Soziolinguistika Klusterra, Topagunea, and Urtxintxa Eskola. 2009. *Gazteen hizkuntza erabileran eragiten duten faktoreen azterketa proiektua. Emaitzen txostena*. N.P.: Soziolinguistika Klusterra.

Terradas. 2009.

Terrades i Saborit, Ignasi. 2004. "La contradicción entre identidad vivida e identificación jurídico-política." *Quaderns de l'Institut Català d'Antropologia* 20: 63–79.

Viviani. 2014.

9

Playing It by Ear: An Introduction to Welshe Strict Metre Poetry

Eurig Salisbury

The elaborately interweaving decorations and illustrations of the famous Book of Kells are icons of Celtic art and culture. These visual manuscript embellishments seem to have been a distinctly Irish feature of the culture, however, for none of the medieval Welsh manuscripts contain anything close to the level of intricate decoration found in the Book of Kells. Nonetheless, what the Welsh manuscripts lack in visual ornamentation, they make up in the complexity of their poetry.

The reason I chose to refer to the famous images of the Kells gospels is because they can be seen as a visual representation of a common phenomenon in Celtic culture—a love of intricate patterns. The visual interweaving in the Irish images is mirrored in the sound of interweaving words, rhymes, and consonants in Welsh poetry. Which is why I have chosen this title for the presentation—in Welsh poetics, the poets are playing it by ear.

By this I mean that the rules of traditional Welsh poetry are governed by what can be heard, and not by what can be seen. This may be an obvious thing to point out in this conference, but the reason I refer to it is because the complexity of the rules may explain why a tradition of improvisation similar to the Basque *bertsolaritza* has not flourished in Wales. Which does not mean that there is no tradition of improvisation in Wales—I will come to that later on—but it will be worth outlining the rules of Welsh poetry before we go any further. It may also better explain why Karen Owen and I went to one side of the stage to compose for twenty minutes on Monday night, while all the other poets improvised on the spot!

Welsh poetry composed in the traditional manner is called *cerdd dafod*, which literally means "tongue craft"/"craft of the tongue." In the Middle Ages, poets performed with musical accompaniment, almost always on the harp, but this aspect of the tradition has been almost completely lost. The manuscripts that safeguarded the poetry have very little to say about the music, unfortunately.

However, traditional poetry is occasionally performed today alongside *cerdd dant*, which means "harp-string craft," a highly complex and relatively recent form of musical accompaniment that is probably quite different to what was used originally by the medieval poets. I should note that *cerdd dant* is rarely used by modern poets—rather their poetry is sung by skilled practitioners of *cerdd dant* and can be performed individually, as a group or even as a choir, almost always with accompaniment on the harp. One other point of interest is that those who sing *cerdd dant* do not follow the melody of the harp; rather, they sing a counter-melody that can be improvised according to the singer's expertise (see https://m.youtube.com/watch?v=zJlcHbLyRc8).

Unlike *cerdd dant*, the rules of *cerdd dafod* have not changed much in about six hundred years. The roots of the craft, however, go back even further to the earliest Welsh poetry, which may belong to the sixth century. What makes *cerdd dafod* unique is the fact that it contains *cynghanedd*, which means roughly "harmony" or "chiming." The underlying principle is that a line of *cynghanedd* sounds good, and creates a certain harmony between words that embellishes a poem when performed.

So, here is a crash-course on the main types of *cynghanedd*.

There are three main types of *cynghanedd*. The simplest type, *cynghanedd lusg* ("trailing"), relies on rhyme alone: a word somewhere in the line rhymes with the accented penult of a final polysyllable:

Mae **arch** | yn Ystrad M**arch**ell

Cynghanedd gytsain ("consonantal") can be divided into three subtypes that reflect varying degrees of strictness. The simplest kind is *cynghanedd draws* ("traversing"), in which the line is divided into two parts (not necessary of equal length) and the consonants in the first half must be matched in the second half, with one consonant or more left out of the correspondence at the beginning of the second half:

Gweiddi | maent am **gywydd**wr

In the next subtype, *cynghanedd groes* ("crossing"), consonants in both halves of the line are matched equally:

Tresbas drud | **tros Bowys draw**

The strictest consonantal subtype is *cynghanedd groes o gyswllt* ("by connection"), in which consonants are "borrowed" from the end of the first half of the line in order to complete the correspondence with the beginning of the line:

O la**wr** E**gwestl** | o**reugall**

All three consonantal subtypes are subject to restrictions governed by the nature of the final word in a line. If the final word is accented, it can only be matched by another accented word at the end of the first half of the line. If the final word is unaccented, it can be matched by either another unaccented or accented word at the end of the first half and, in both cases, the consonants on the penult in the final word in the line must correspond in the matching word in the first half:

Da fu'r gwŷr, | **difyr gariad**

In all but a very few cases, the final consonants (if any) in both words must be different, otherwise they form a rhyme or a *proest* ("partial rhyme").

The third type of *cynghanedd* relies on both rhyme and consonance. In *cynghanedd sain* ("sonorous"), the line is divided into three: the first two parts rhyme with one another and the third part is in consonance (of varying degrees of strictness) with the second:

Ym mynwent | **c**wfent | a'u **c**ell

This is an example of the most common form of *cynghanedd sain*, in which the final word in the line is accented and the metrically emphasized word in the second part of the line is unaccented (a combination that does not occur in *cynghanedd gytsain*). In this case, the consonants on the penult in the second part of the line do not have to match the final consonants in the third part. If the final word in the line is unaccented, the same rules apply as in *cynghanedd gystain*, namely that the consonants on the penult in the word in the second part of the line (whether accented or unaccented) must correspond:

Teg | a **difr**eg | yw **dwyfr**on
Ar fardd | y **ch**war**dd** | a **cherdd**awr

There are no limits on the number of syllables in a line of *cynghanedd*, but traditional metres can contain any number between four and ten, with seven syllables being the most common. So-called forbidden faults and exceptions to the rules of *cynghanedd* are too numerous to detail here.

I hope you can now see why Karen Owen and I had to take our time on Monday night! All these rules make it quite difficult to improvise poetry in *cynghanedd*. However, modern poets do occasionally take part in competitions that require a degree of improvisation. Before I turn to those competitions, I should mention a few medieval examples that seem to suggest that improvisation has always played a small part in Welsh poetry.

Some bardic grammars found in the manuscripts seem to suggest that medieval poets could improvise in repeat performances of a poem. In other words, the poet would perform a poem for the first time, very probably after prior composition, and then in later performances of the same poem, some variation could come into play as the poet improvised the old material to suit a different audience. This suggests that the poets were capable of creating and recreating complex lines of *cynghanedd* in a very short period of time. It is not surprising, perhaps, that professional poets who dedicated their time to the business of composing poetry day in day out could occasionally turn their hand to improvisation.

This theory is supported by occasional stories found in the manuscripts, written alongside the poetry, that seem to explain the circumstances in which some poems were composed. One such story is found with a late fourteenth-century poem by a poet called Sypyn Cyfeiliog, who was travelling one winter's night to the home of his patron. He was thrown off course, however, by a terrible snowstorm, and was forced to abandon his route and take shelter at the home of another patron. This patron's house was already full of visiting poets and musicians, whose poems of praise were well-prepared for a Christmas feast the following day. Sypyn Cyfeiliog had likewise prepared a poem for his original patron, but now felt ashamed that he didn't have a poem for the man who had given him shelter. It would bring shame on him as a poet to turn up at the feast the next day without a poem of praise for his generous patron, so he decided to stay up all night composing a long and intricate new poem. According to the story, Sypyn Cyfeiliog succeeded in finishing his poem on time and wowed his audience, who considered his poem to be superior to any other at the Christmas feast.

This poem is accordingly called a *cerdd unnos*, or "a one-night poem," and other poems are referred to in the same way in the manuscripts, usually because the poet had apparently turned up at a patron's house without a poem. Another reason for composing a one-nighter was the sudden illness of a patron who quickly needed the poet's assistance.

As well as these occasional *cerddi unnos*, improvisation of a more formal nature is also mentioned in the manuscripts. One rather strange custom popular in both the fifteenth and sixteenth centuries was the *cyff clêr*, or "the poets' butt of ridicule." This custom took place during wedding feasts, which seem to have been held over a number of consecutive nights. On the first night, any number of poets would turn up to the celebrations, and one poet was chosen to be the butt of ridicule. This poet was usually the most prominent in the group, a widely respected figure whose satirising was all the more effective because of it. The other poets then invented a lewd story about this poet, a fabrication or embellishment that may have nonetheless included a grain of truth.

For example, the earliest example of the genre is a story about a well-known poet called Tudur Penllyn, who was apparently crossing a mountain one day when he was attacked by a wolf, and the wolf bit his testicles off. The other poets all composed poems ridiculing Tudur Penllyn, including his own son, Ieuan, who mourned the fact that he had never have any more brothers of sisters! The themes often revolved around masculinity and fertility, which may explain why the custom was held at a wedding feast. After enduring these satirical poems, the object of their ridicule—the poor poet—was expected to compose a poem in response by the following day. This show of expertise in improvisation by the master poet was a way of reasserting his predominance, for by dazzling everyone with his new poem he would succeed in putting the minor poets back in their place.

This rather bizarre custom has not survived to today—thankfully, perhaps! Nevertheless, the custom of composing poetry in a short period of time continues in a competition known as the *ymryson*, which means "duel." In its most traditional form, this is a competition in which the poets turn up—usually at a festival—without much prior arrangement, and spontaneously form teams of usually four poets. They are then given four or five tasks which they must complete within about thirty minutes. The poems are read aloud in turn, after which they are evaluated by an expert—usually a respected poet—and given marks out of ten. The winning team are sometimes presented with a cup and occasionally a small amount of prize money.

The *ymryson* differs from two other popular competitions as it is the only competition that involves improvisation from beginning to end. The *talwrn* competition, which means "cockpit," is very similar to the *ymryson*, except that the teams of poets are formed and given tasks at least a week before the event. A very popular and long-running *talwrn* competition is broadcast annually on BBC Radio Cymru. My team, Y Glêr, has won the competition twice, first in 2012 and most recently in 2017. Although different from the *ymryson*, this competition does have a small element of improvisation—one of the tasks in every round is to complete within a minute a couplet of traditional metre after being given one line by the adjudicator.

The other popular competition is the *stomp*, a recent development in Welsh poetry in which poets compete individually by reading a poem composed beforehand, and then the audience votes with coloured paper for their favourite poem. The successful poets then go head-to-head by reading a second poem in the final round, and the winning poet is given a milking stool. This prize reflects the informal nature of the *stomp*—in which some poets sometimes read very obscene or risqué work—because the milking stool itself is a send-up of the most prestigious prize in Welsh poetry—the Chair, which is awarded to the creator of a winning composition at an *eisteddfod* (cultural festival).

The complexity of *cynghanedd*, therefore, has not always been a barrier to improvisation in Welsh poetry, although that small degree of improvisation pales, of course, in comparison to the complexity of the Basque tradition. Nonetheless, there is much to be said and indeed gained from further investigation into similarities and differences between both traditions, especially in terms of genre manipulation and the relationship between poets and their audiences, not to mention the important roles that poetry can play in the cultures of minority languages.

> Gall Cymru gyfrif prifeirdd,
> Gwlad y Basg all **glywed** beirdd!

> (Wales can count its poets,
> but the Basques can hear theirs!)

About the Contributors

After graduating in Basque Philology at the University of the Basque Country (EHU), **Miren Artetxe Sarasola** did a Master's Degree in Cognitive and Linguistic Sciences at the University of Barcelona. She is currently PhD student at the Department of Audiovisual Communication and Advertising in EHU as well as being member of the NOR and Feminist Anthropology research groups. Her research fields include oral improvisation, sociolinguistics and anthropology. She is a bertsolari.

Albert Casals Ibañez is a member of the research group Música, Veu i Educació. He has a PhD in the Didactics of Music. His thesis treatedimprovised verses and their educational use in Catalonia. He promotes the inter-school project Corrandescola, based on the didactic use of improvised verses at school. He is also the author of *Corrandescola: Proposta didactica per treballar la glosa a Primària*. He regularly publishes articles in Catalan, Spanish and international magazines.

Ruth Finngegan is an anthropologist and Emeritus Professor of Social Sciences at The Open University (United Kingdom). She is an expert on oral literature, and started by researching the oral culture creations in Africa and the South Pacific, having made a great contribution to the recognition of Oral Literature as a literary genre. She covers various areas of research on comparative sociology/anthropology of artistic performances (mainly on oral culture creations and music), communication and oral performance.

Josep Vincent Frechina is a researcher specialized in music and popular culture of the Mediterranean countries. He is editor of *Caramella* magazine (1999-present) and he often contributes articles to other media as well. He is author of the books La cançó en valencià: *Dels repertoris tradicionals als gèneres moderns* (Acadèmia Valenciana de la Llengua, 2011) and *Pensar en vers: La cançó improvisada als països de la Mediterrània* (Llibres de Caramella, 2013).

Jone M. Hernandez is professor of Social Anthropology at the University of the Basque Country. She has studied Basque, Basque culture, youth, leisure and sports, mainly from the perspective of gender and feminist theory. Currently she studies the emotions and the corporal aspects.

Thierry Rougier is a member of the Passages Joint Research Unit. Regarding cultural anthropology and musicology, he has focused his research on the poets-singers from Brazil. He defended his thesis in 2006: "Los Cantadores, improvising poets from the Northeast of Brazil." He has published articles in collaboration with the Occitan Research Center CORDAE/La Talvera de Cordes-sur-Ciel. His areas of interest include cultural and linguistic diversity, world music, and guitars and guitarists. He is also director of the festival "Atypical Nights" celebrated in Sud-Gironde.

Eurig Salisbury is a poet and lecturer in creative writing at the Department of Welsh and Celtic Studies in Aberystwyth University. He was Bardd Plant Cymru, 2011–2013 (Welsh children's laureate) and was one of the Hay Festival's International Fellows, 2012–2013. His first collection of poetry, *Llyfr Glas Eurig* (Eurig's blue book) was published in 2008.

Patricia Tapanes Suárez graduated in sociology at the University of Havana. She carried out her post-graduate work on the identity of Cuba and cultural anthropology. She has taken part in many projects such as the Specialized Workshops for Children's Repent (throughout the country), promoted by the Ministry of Culture in Cuba. She has done researched on the social aspect and the symbolism of improvised verse singing, and, as a result, she has collaborated in a multitude of documentaries and albums of Cuban popular culture and orality.

Harkaitz Zubiri is a PhD in Sociology, he also has a Bachelor's Degree in English Philology and

Sociology. He is holder of a diploma in Teaching Foreign Languages as well. He is currently a researcher and professor at the University of the Basque Country. One of his main fields of research is culture in Basque, a subject on which he has published articles and books. He has recently finished a sociological study on bertsolaritza. Besides, he is author of a novel and a nonfiction book.

CPSIA information can be obtained
at www.ICGtesting.com
Printed in the USA
FSHW021318251118
53897FS